TEAR DOWN THIS WALL
OF SILENCE

TEAR DOWN THIS WALL
OF SILENCE

Dealing with Sexual Abuse in Our Churches

(an introduction for those who will hear)

DALE INGRAHAM
with rebecca davis

AMBASSADOR INTERNATIONAL
GREENVILLE, SOUTH CAROLINA & BELFAST, NORTHERN IRELAND

www.ambassador-international.com

Tear Down This Wall
Of Silence

ISBN: 978-1-62020-521-1
eISBN: 978-1-62020-428-3

Cover Design & Page Layout by Hannah Nichols

This publication includes personal stories by abuse survivors, used by permission. Inquiries can be directed to Ambassador International.

Adapted and enhanced from an earlier version of this work, *Tear Down This Wall: Sexual Abuse Within the Church*, by Dale Ingraham, 2012.

AMBASSADOR INTERNATIONAL
Emerald House
427 Wade Hampton Blvd.
Greenville, SC 29609, USA
www.ambassador-international.com

AMBASSADOR BOOKS
The Mount
2 Woodstock Link
Belfast, BT6 8DD, Northern Ireland, UK
www.ambassadormedia.co.uk

The colophon is a trademark of Ambassador

DEDICATION

To my wife, Faith,

and all those who have known the pain of abuse.

Faith has been a great wife and mom

and a true "help meet" for me in over thirty years of ministry.

Since 2008 I have enjoyed partnering with her

in Speaking Truth in Love Ministries

as we speak in churches, Bible colleges,

and wherever God gives us an open door.

CONTENTS

PART ONE
KNOW WHAT YOU'RE DEALING WITH

CHAPTER 1
RECOGNIZE THE SIN IN OUR MIDST

CHAPTER 2
UNDERSTAND THE VICTIMS

CHAPTER 3

UNDERSTAND THE OFFENDERS

CHAPTER 4

FACE THE REPERCUSSIONS OF THE SIN

CHAPTER 5

UNDERSTAND THE ENABLERS

PART TWO

STOP THE WRONG THINKING
BELIEVE AND SPEAK THE TRUTH

CHAPTER 6

TEAR DOWN THIS WALL OF
WRONG THINKING

PART THREE
TAKE RESPONSIBILITY AND ACTION

CHAPTER 10
WHAT OUR CHURCHES MUST DO

CHAPTER 11

WHAT THE OFFENDER MUST DO

CHAPTER 12

HOW FAMILY AND FRIENDS MUST HELP

CHAPTER 13

THE ABUSE SURVIVOR'S SHEPHERD

CHAPTER 14
VOICES OF GRIEF, VOICES OF HOPE

ACKNOWLEDGEMENTS

I especially want to thank my wife, Faith, whose journey of abuse and healing was one of the reasons that I set out to write this book.

I appreciate my church family, who gives me the time to advocate for those who are abused.

Boz Tchividjian has pioneered work in the area of independent investigations regarding abuse. His support and input have been a big encouragement.

A special thank you to Rebecca Davis, without whom this book would never have been finished. Her passion for helping those who are abused and her amazing writing and editing abilities are inspiring.

Special thanks also go to Cheryl Childers, MSW, LISW-CP; Rachelle Harris, childhood sexual abuse survivor; and advocate Kristi Wetzel, all of whom read the entire manuscript and gave much valuable input.

Many anonymous abuse survivors graciously allowed their voices to speak out on these pages. To all of them, to all other abuse survivors and advocates who are standing up to protect others, may God grant us victory in breaking the cycle of abuse.

FOREWORDS

BASYLE "BOZ" TCHIVIDJIAN

Founder and Executive Director, Godly Response to
Abuse in the Christian Environment (GRACE)

Many years ago as a prosecutor, God opened my eyes to the horrific realities of child sexual abuse. As I prepared cases for prosecution, I encountered many precious souls that had given up all hope as a result of being victimized as a child. What I found even more disturbing was the reality that this dark and destructive crime has no boundaries and is epidemic in size within the Christian community.

Why has the church been so silent about a sin that is destroying its community one soul at a time? In fact, far too often when child sexual abuse is discussed within the Protestant community, it is in the context of pointing the finger at our Catholic brothers and sisters. This is sadly the way Protestant churches have been able to avoid addressing this darkness within their very own soul.

Clinical psychologist Mary Gail Frawley-O'Dea said, "The more profound the betrayal and the more vital to survival the betrayer is, the more likely it is that the trauma will be denied, dissociated, or diminished by both the victim and the bystander who consciously or unconsciously insist on maintaining an attachment to the victimizer on whom they depend for some aspect of survival, including at times spiritual survival." This quotation has immensely helped me understand the failure of the Christian community to confront and address a sin that is prevalent and destructive. Christians too often deny, dissociate, or diminish this crime because we have elevated the perpetrators and the institutions to a position that can be filled only by the righteous and holy God. When survivors come forward, the institution often feels threatened and immediately moves to protect the "godly" perpetrator, while at the same time devaluing and demoralizing the very souls that need to be loved and embraced.

I believe this monumental failure on the part of the Christian community is a consequence of its failure to understand and embrace the gospel. The gospel tells us that it is Christ's perfection, Christ's obedience, Christ's holiness, Christ's selflessness (the list could go on and on and on) that reconcile dark and depraved sinners such as you and me with a perfect, sovereign, and loving God. Put another way, it is the "good works" of Jesus, not us, that draw us into the arms of our Heavenly Father. The consequence of fully grasping and embracing this indescribable truth is that we discover that our identity is not in ourselves and what we do, but in Christ and what He has done. Therefore, when we seek to control and protect the institution, we display that we have failed to understand the very fundamentals of the gospel. This control and protectionism is often carried out under the guise of "protecting the integrity of the gospel," when in reality it is nothing more than protecting the identity and reputation of the institution.

Perhaps the most common method of such protectionism is secrecy and silence. An institutional-centered church will do all it can to silence those who expose sin in order to protect its "reputation within the community." A Gospel-centered church will embrace light and be transparent about sin. It will also lovingly embrace those wounded by sin, regardless of what others may think or say, understanding that its identity and reputation is in Christ alone.

Seldom do we encounter saints who are willing to give up status, reputation, and even wealth in order to bring light to a dark area of the Christian world. Martin Luther, William Wilberforce, and Dietrich Bonhoeffer are just a few that come to mind. Another such saint is Dale Ingraham. I was blessed to have the opportunity to meet Dale and Faith Ingraham at a conference. I was immediately struck by the burden God has placed upon their hearts to carry a bright light to a very dark and quiet place within the church. As a pastor and husband, Dale has witnessed the evils of child sexual abuse within the Christian community. He has witnessed how perpetrators within our churches will use and exploit Scripture and biblical truths in carrying out their horrors upon little children. He has witnessed time and time again the utter silence of the church in refusing to confront and respond to this grave sin. He has also witnessed the lifelong emotional, physical, and spiritual damage caused by such victimization, and the church's failure to respond with gospel-centered excellence.

Far too many others have also witnessed such horrors and have responded by simply giving up and walking away in anger and dismay. I would be lying if I told you that Dale doesn't get angry and dismayed at how many within the Christian community have turned their backs on this epidemic; however, he has not walked away. Dale's love for our great and gracious God and his precious little ones has propelled him to walk toward the church with a message that it must hear and embrace. A message that says the days of silence and secrecy surrounding sexual abuse are over, and the days of light and transparency have begun.

This is a message that many abuse survivors have been waiting their entire lives to hear. Tragically, it is also a message that many within the church continue to ignore, sometimes vilifying those who bring it, including Dale and Faith Ingraham. *Tear Down This Wall of Silence* is a book that will clearly bring this powerful gospel-centered message to all who will read it. Dale helps us understand the complicated dynamics of sexual abuse within our churches in order that we all may be better equipped to bring this same message to our respective faith communities. He also provides a comprehensive overview of the many reasons the church often prefers darkness and secrecy to light and transparency.

Perhaps the most powerful punch of this book is that it is written by one who has not simply studied the subject, but whose life has been dramatically impacted by all he has seen and experienced.

Supreme Court Justice William Brandeis once said, "Sunshine is the best disinfectant." The only way that we will begin to see transformation within the Christian community in how it understands, confronts, and responds to this dark sin is to bring it to light. Ultimately, it is the light of Christ that will shatter the silence and secrecy and bring healing not only to hurting souls, but also to hurting institutions. I praise my friend and my brother for carrying this bright torch into the darkness.

You are not alone. There is hope.

BASYLE J. TCHIVIDJIAN

JEFF CRIPPEN

Pastor and author of *A Cry for Justice: How the Evil of
Domestic Abuse Hides in Your Church!*

Only a few days ago I was at a beach on the Pacific Ocean not far
from where my wife and I live. It was an unusually spectacular win-
ter day with no wind and temperatures in the mid-sixties. The white
sand beach, normally deserted this time of year, was crowded with
families and people of all sorts. Everyone was having a fine time. All
appeared well. It was anything but.

At the edge of a very steep mountain of sand, three children were
happily digging caves with their hands, crawling headfirst inside in
order to dig deeper. One girl, about nine years old, was inside her
cave with only her legs sticking out. And the people, the adults, probably fifty or more of them in the immediate area, just stood around,
watching the waves, looking at the sights, and having a good old time.

Anyone who lives in this area knows full well, or should know if
they ever read a newspaper, that children die with some frequency
when they are buried in these sand caves they dig. The girl was in
fact digging her own grave. If she continued to tunnel, I assure you
that she was going to die. And I told her so. I went up to her (there
were no parents anywhere to be seen) and said, "You are going to
die if you keep digging." She looked at me with some sheepishness,
taken aback, I think, that a stranger, and an old guy at that, had issued
her such a warning. I explained to her and her friends about tunnel
cave-ins and how it is impossible for a person buried by the sand to
get themselves out.

I watched. In a few minutes she was back in her cave digging away. Not one of the many adults in the area noted her or said a word to her, until one unusual lady spied the girl while still about 75 yards away. The woman pointed and started toward the cave, and as she came by me, I said, "You see the danger, right?" She saw. I told her I had warned the girl, but to no avail. This wise lady would have none of it. "She is going to listen to me!"

And the girl did. The woman, willing to create a scene on a pleasant, sunny day at the beach, sounded the warning. As she walked away, she looked at me and said, "Thank you for validating me."

What I have just described is what this book is about. Dale Ingraham (along with his wife, Faith) is calling upon the Christian church to open its eyes and see that what we think is a fun-filled, refreshing, sunny day at the beach – isn't. Many pastors, elders, and church members are like those people I saw that day standing around on the beach, oblivious to the imminent danger at hand that was about to kill a child. *Tear Down This Wall of Silence* is a shout to slumbering, complacent Christians living in denial to wake up and see what is lurking among them. And it is more.

Dale Ingraham maintains that the wickedness of sexual abuse in the Christian church is able to hide and thrive because of silence. It isn't simply that Christians are ignorant of this evil. Though this is sometimes the case, in most cases churches are willfully ignorant and blind to it. The silence proves it. The silence is willful.

The people I saw that day on the beach had to have seen what that little girl was doing, but they chose to be blind to it. *Tear Down This Wall of Silence* shouts at such people to open their eyes, expose the wickedness that works to creep in among Christ's people, and shine the light of God's truth on it so brightly that it can no longer hide or even exist in our pews.

This book is for pastors, elders, church members, parents, youth groups, and all Christians. It contains practical advice about sexual predators, about their methods, about the damage they effect upon their victims, the hope that these victims can find in Christ, and perhaps most of all, it is a book about the ungodly silence that denies and enables the evil among us.

The Ingrahams are people peculiarly prepared by the Lord to sound this warning. They have suffered the pain and trauma of sexual abuse. They have personally felt the intense pressure that is put upon victims to just "be quiet" about what happened. But as this book demonstrates, they resolved before God that they would tear down the wall of silence and shout from the rooftops what had happened to them and who had done it.

May the Lord richly bless Dale and Faith for their courage and faithfulness, and may we all join them in being silent no more.

JEFF CRIPPEN

INTRODUCTION

"Mr. Gorbachev, tear down this wall." I remember those words well. I was a young man pastoring in my first church when President Ronald Reagan said them. I remember the feeling of pride in my country and my president. I was inspired by his courage and determination to change the evils that faced his presidency and our nation.

The Berlin Wall was more than just a symbol of oppression. It divided families, institutions, economics, countries, and a way of life. On one side was light, truth, freedom, and the ability to grow; on the other, darkness, deceit, oppression, and stagnation. It's hard to describe the excitement we felt as we watched crowds gather on both sides of the wall, with each person testing the resolve of the Soviet Union's grip on power and its decades-long isolation from the rest of the world.

Another wall still stands today that is far greater and more menacing than the Berlin Wall, and it is not constructed by the Soviet empire. It has been constructed by many in the church. It's not a wall of concrete and steel but of silence and secrecy. It's not guarded by soldiers with guns but by church leaders with Bibles. Those who dare to climb over this wall aren't shot but are shamed and betrayed by the very ones who should be protecting them.

This is a partition that has been long in the making and was built to hide one of the greatest evils in our world, the raping and molesting of vulnerable souls to satisfy a perverted lust in the hearts of many offenders. Sadly, many of our church leaders continue the tradition of maintaining and protecting this wall of silence and secrecy to try to conceal the sexual abuse of children and others from the efforts of those who want to tear it down. Keeping the wall of silence and secrecy in place allows them to avoid dealing with the sin and the aftermath of the abuse.

Predators go where they can find prey, and all too often it is in our churches. Like the Berlin Wall, this wall of secrecy was built and remains in place primarily for two reasons: to keep some people in and to keep other people out. Religious organizations use this wall to keep the sin hidden, because without it the sin is exposed to the public.

The Berlin Wall was obvious and visible. This wall of silence, on the other hand, is subtle and invisible. The Berlin Wall surrounded a city, but the wall of silence surrounds a sin.

It's time to challenge Christians everywhere. Tear down this wall!

CAUTION

FOR SEXUAL ABUSE SURVIVORS

You may have picked up this book hoping for answers to questions you've mulled over for years. This book is written for you and for the Christian community to hear survivors' voices loud and clear. I pray that they will have the ears to hear.

Please be sure to practice self-care while reading through this book.

The gray italicized sections are areas you might want to skip and come back to at a later date, or read with a friend or counselor. These are survivors' stories, which may be very similar to your own. They were brave enough to share parts of their stories because they want to be an encouragement to you and other survivors who will read their accounts.

Because everyone's experience and healing journey is different, you may find other areas of this book particularly triggering as well. Chapters 3 and 11 are about the offender. Please take special care while reading these chapters.

If your abuser used Bible verses, or if the Bible was used in counseling in ways that re-traumatized you, then some of the Scriptures you read here that are meant to give reassurance about God's love may instead cause a sense of panic. This may be a good time to work through some of these Scriptures with a wise counselor who will patiently help you process without any shame or blame.

Please protect yourself from triggers and dissociation. Keep yourself safe by putting the book down if you feel these begin to come on. Take a break and walk outside. Perhaps read this book during the day rather than in the dark of night. You are valuable and worthy of protection and safety. We at Speaking Truth in Love Ministries love you and are praying for you.

PART ONE

KNOW WHAT YOU'RE DEALING WITH

CHAPTER 1

RECOGNIZE THE SIN IN OUR MIDST

A SHOCKING REVELATION

I sat in the car in uncomfortable silence. Agonizing silence.

Faith, my girlfriend, stared straight ahead at the dashboard. She twisted the tissue in her hand, ignoring the tears falling into her lap.

"It would be better . . . if we just ended it here . . ." Her voice came in short bursts, so quiet that I had to strain to hear.

She knew our relationship was becoming serious. She knew I had thought about wanting to ask her to marry me. But we both also knew we had hit a wall in our relationship. Something was keeping us from being able to draw close with each other.

"It's too hard . . . I can't do it . . . It would be better if we just didn't get close."

"But what is it?" I pressed gently. Then I had an idea. "Has somebody hurt you?"

Another agonizing pause.

"Yes." She looked down at that torn tissue, her voice barely audible. "I was abused . . . sexually." She lifted her hand and covered her face as she said that word. "Someone close. A relative."

One of her uncles had molested her? I knew so little about these things.

"It will be all right," I whispered with determination. "We'll work through it."

She nodded, her eyes tight shut, and wiped her face with the scrap of tissue.

Over the next months we tried to talk about the issue in bits and pieces. She wanted to tell me more. I wanted to show her that I loved her no matter what. I was only twenty-two and wasn't sure what was involved in helping someone who had been sexually abused, but I felt sure that if I just showed her how much I loved her and cared for her, everything would be all right.

It was 1982, and we were in Bible college. Faculty and staff who loved God were all around us. Why didn't we go to anyone for help?

Maybe because in all my life I had never heard anyone talk about such things. I had grown up in a Christian home, gone to Christian school, gone to church all my life, and was now in Bible college. All kinds of difficult issues were being discussed. But sexual abuse was never, ever mentioned. The wall that had hindered my relationship with the girl I loved still stood, foreboding but invisible, in the society in which I moved, without my even realizing it.

Shortly before I asked her to marry me, Faith made another revelation. I waited as she took one deep breath after another. Finally she spoke.

"It was my father."

Her father?

Her pastor father?

WE STILL DIDN'T KNOW

By 2005 Faith and I had been married for over twenty years. I had also been a pastor for over twenty years as well, but still had received no teaching on sexual abuse and the extent of its presence in our society and our churches. I knew that my Baptist pastor father-in-law had committed sexual abuse, but somehow I still thought that sexual abuse as a "problem" was distant from us, removed from us. It was the stuff of news reports of stranger-rape. It was an issue out in the world, or in the Catholic church. Not in our churches.

For all these years, Faith and I only occasionally spoke about her own abuse, and never about the larger issue. Both of us had many misconceptions and a great deal of ignorance.

In 2005 all this began to change. Faith began to read books about abuse and to tell me what she was learning. We were both shocked to discover a dark underworld of sexual abuse in the churches, hidden in plain sight.

THE STARTLING STATISTICS

I had thought that most sexual assaults were committed by strangers, but nothing could be further from the truth. The Abel and

Harlow Child Molestation Prevention Study of 2001 says that 90% of child molesters molest children that they already know.[1] Furthermore, most molesters are in a position of authority over the victim. It may be an older family member, a babysitter, a youth leader, a pastor, a deacon, a daycare worker, a boss at work, a scout leader, a teacher, a boyfriend, or other perceived authority, who then uses this position to take advantage of the victim to gratify his desire for sexual pleasure as well as for power and control.[2]

Several studies have indicated that as many as one in three girls and one in six boys will be raped or molested by the time they're 18 years old.[3] Studies show that 18-20% of young women will be sexually assaulted during their college years.[4] Furthermore, statistics show that only 3% of these cases of abuse ever reach a conviction.[5]

These are shocking statistics, and when we quote them, we're often met with incredulity. For example, Faith and I shared these statistics with a missionary couple. At first they were shocked, but after thinking about it, they said that among the people they work with, sexual assault might be nearly 100% of the girls.

---

1   Abel and Harlow study cited on Child Molestation Research & Prevention Institute website, cmrpi.org, at http://www.cmrpi.org/pdfs/study.pdf.

2   For an excellent and thorough treatment of the power dynamic in sexual abuse, see "Sexual Abuse of Power," by Michal Buchhandler-Raphael, *University of Florida Journal of Law & Public Policy*, April 1, 2010, pp. 77-146.

3   J. Briere and D. M. Eliot, "Prevalence and Psychological Sequence of Self-Reported Childhood Physical and Sexual Abuse in General Population." *Child Abuse & Neglect*, 2003, Vol. 27, Issue 10, pp. 1205–1222.

4   Glenn Kessler, "One in five women in college sexually assaulted: the source of this statistic," *The Washington Post*, May 1, 2014, accessed via http://www.washingtonpost.com/blogs/fact-checker/wp/2014/05/01/one-in-five-women-in-college-sexually-assaulted-the-source-of-this-statistic/.

5   The website of the Rape, Abuse, and Incest National Network (RAINN) displays many disturbing statistics. You can see them at www.rainn.org/statistics.

When I gave this information to a man in a large Christian ministry, his tone changed from polite to impatient, claiming that those figures were way too extreme. Later, we saw that the website of his own ministry displayed the identical statistics. Even though the evidence was fully available to him, he was unaware of the magnitude of the problem.

WHY IS IT SUCH A BIG DEAL?

A simple Internet search will reveal that dozens of books and scores of websites have been written simply to help sexual abuse survivors heal from the trauma of their abuse. This trauma can include recurring nightmares, dissociation, sudden flashbacks into the event, a desperate desire for suicide, dissociative identity disorder, and other symptoms of post-traumatic stress disorder.[6] Sexual abuse affects not only the survivor, but the survivor's marriage and children, as well as our churches and society as a whole. Chapter 2 further explores the far-reaching effects of sexual abuse.

BUT NOT IN OUR CHRISTIAN MINISTRIES!

Even though research indicates that most sexual abuse takes place in the home, news reports constantly remind us that such abuse is also found in churches and other Christian ministries.[7] Shortly after becoming the new pastor of a church, Bill Anderson found himself in the middle of a pastor's worst nightmare. Over sixty children had

---

6   For more information on the effects of sexual abuse, see Diane Langberg, Ph.D., *Counseling Survivors of Sexual Abuse* (Xulon Press, 2003), especially chapters 5, 8, 12, 20, and 21.

7   Sometimes the two are the same, since a pastor may be molesting his own daughter or son. Sometimes there is overlap, since a church member may go to church leadership to try to report abuse that is happening at home.

been sexually molested in the nursery by two older boys. Even as the facts were coming out about the abuse, it was hard for many to believe. One woman in particular raised her hand during the informational meeting and said, "This didn't really happen in our church, did it?" Anderson says, "It was overwhelming to think of children being raped, sodomized, forced into oral sex, beaten, and threatened right around the corner from where she was singing hymns and reading her Bible."[8]

Tragically, even many pastors and other church leaders have been found guilty of the offense of sexual abuse,[9] and those who turn a blind eye are denying reality. This abuse by church leaders is especially evil, because the violation is taking place at the hands of those who are entrusted with a responsibility to lead and protect the sheep. It is particularly abominable when one who should have been a protector has become the predator.

Christian psychologist Dr. Diane Langberg has lamented the fact that so few keep their ears and eyes open to the problem of abuse. "[M]any in the church do not believe that abuse of any kind has touched so many lives. That means it is kept secret because many [abuse survivors] fear they will not be believed. Attention to the problem is not a priority because the problem is believed to be rare."[10]

When Faith and I started Speaking Truth in Love Ministries, we thought that we were the only ones trying to educate churches

---

8   Bill Anderson, *When Child Abuse Comes to Church: Recognizing Its Occurrence and What to Do About It.* (Minneapolis: Bethany House, 1992), p. 55.

9   The news is filled with examples. A recent one involves the case of youth worker Nathaniel Morales at Covenant Life Church of Gaithersburg, Maryland, which can be accessed at http://www.wjla.com/articles/2014/05/nathaniel-morales-of-covenant-life-church-convicted-of-sexually-abusing-young-boys-103175.html

10   Langberg, *Counseling Survivors of Sexual Abuse*, p. 284.

about sexual abuse. But since then we've found dozens of other organizations who have similar ministries. One of them is GRACE, Godly Response to Abuse in the Christian Environment,[11] founded by Professor Basyle "Boz" Tchividjian, a law professor at Liberty University and former child abuse prosecutor. When GRACE was asked to investigate a missionary boarding school where sexual abuse had been alleged, they found that not only had extensive sexual abuse been perpetrated, but it also had been ignored or actively covered up by some of the former leaders of the mission. Soon after the investigation, Professor Tchividjian stated,

> In the history of the church, there are few, if any, instances of organized religion taking seriously its responsibility to protect children from abuse. In the abstract, of course, the church is always opposed to the physical, sexual, and emotional violation of a child's body and mind. When faced with the reality of abuse, however, the church is slow to side with the victim and quick to protect the perpetrator. In doing so, the church inflicts further pain on the child, and emboldens the perpetrator in his or her sin.[12]

In her book *This Little Light: Beyond a Baptist Preacher Predator and His Gang,* Christa Brown tells how as a young girl, she wanted to be a missionary. But after being sexually assaulted by the youth pastor, her whole world changed. The music minister in whom she confided told her not to tell anyone, so she obediently kept the wall of silence

---

11   www.netgrace.org.

12   "Amended GRACE Report on NTM Fanda," p. 66. This can be viewed at https://www.scribd.com/doc/36559323/Amended-GRACE-Report-on-NTM-Fanda-Amended-Edition.

in place for years. Years later, when Christa became concerned that the youth pastor might be molesting others, she found that no one would help her—not even the music minister she had confided in. They wanted her to remain behind the wall of silence so that she wouldn't embarrass the church.[13] Jeff Crippen, in response to this story, wrote these scathing words:

> If one quality in every real Christian is this hunger and thirst for righteousness, how then is it possible for a Christian to pervert justice and to oppose righteousness as these men did in [Christa] Brown's case? The thing is impossible. To such men, we must say no less than, "Woe to you, scribes, Pharisees, hypocrites!" Does that seem too harsh? Then consider that Brown's denomination knowingly permitted her rapist to continue as a children's minister for years![14]

LET'S OWN THE PROBLEM

In 2006 Faith and I founded Speaking Truth in Love Ministries to help churches deal with this sin of sexual abuse within our Christian ministries, because we can't have a meaningful impact in the world until this sin is dealt with in our own midst.

Many abuse survivor websites display stories of pain and suffering caused by the very ones that were supposed to care for the weak and vulnerable.[15] When Christians take an honest look at the condi-

---

13   Christa Brown, *This Little Light: Beyond a Baptist Preacher Predator and His Gang* (Cedarburg, WI: Foremost Press, 2009).

14   Jeff Crippen and Anna Wood, *A Cry for Justice: How the Evil of Domestic Abuse Hides in Your Church!* (Greenville, SC: Calvary Press Publishing, 2012), pp. 168-169.

15   For examples, see www.mksafetynet.net, www.bangladeshmksspeak. wordpress.com, www.fandaeagles.com, www.snapnetwork.org, and www.stop-baptistpredators.org.

tion of our churches and missions programs, we must be sickened at the reality that many of the ones supposedly sent by God to care for the sheep are in fact destroying them. It is not only outside the church, but in the church as well, a tragic epidemic.

In Joshua 7, Achan took something that God never intended him to have and buried it under his tent. Achan's sin caused great pain for his family, cost the lives of many soldiers, and eventually cost his own life. Only after Joshua and Israel as a nation dealt with Achan's sin did God once again bless his people. There are those who claim the holy name of Christ, who attend churches across the country, who, like Achan, take what is not theirs and then bury it where no one sees. Many churches may have buried beneath them "the accursed thing."

We as Christians can forget that God says in 2 Chronicles 7:14, "If my people who are called by my name will humble themselves, and pray and seek my face, and turn from their wicked ways, then I will hear from heaven, and will forgive their sin and heal their land." So often Christians will blame an ungodly world or even the victims for the problems in society, but God tells His own people to turn from "their wicked ways." We need to be willing to examine the horrific evils hiding in our midst.

HOW SHOULD WE DEAL WITH IT?

The initial sin is the offender's, but by protecting the offender and rejecting the victim, other people become an accessory to his sin. Proverbs 17:15 says, "He who justifies the wicked, and he who condemns the just, both of them alike are an abomination to the Lord." When believers protect offenders from the law, they justify their evil deeds, and when believers reject the cries of the abused, they in effect condemn the just.

Tear Down This Wall of Silence points Christians in the direction of loving action. People who love God need to understand the ramifications of the sin and the dynamics of the offender, the victim, and the enablers (Part One); we need to believe and speak the truth about sin, forgiveness, mercy, justice, grace, and love (Part Two); and we need to take responsibility and action (Part Three).

While revival is happening in other places around the world, much of the Western church languishes in frustration and fruitlessness. Though there are many reasons for this, the secret sin of sexual abuse is surely a major one. When it comes to this sin, it appears that the church has a blind spot. The world sees it, the victims see it, and the advocates for victims see it, but many in our churches don't see it. It's as if many Christians are blind to what is happening all around them. Proverbs 28:13 advises, "He who covers his sins will not prosper, but whoever confesses and forsakes them will have mercy." We, the church, want God's mercy and blessing. We must be willing to confess and forsake this glaring sin.

Christians in America: It's time for us all to stop the denial. For too long we've said that this evil happens only outside of "our" church. For too long we've minimized the crime. For too long we've protected offenders. It's time for the body of Christ to speak the whole truth about this sin. It's time to tear down the wall of silence.

CHAPTER 2

UNDERSTAND THE VICTIMS

A single incident of any type of sexual abuse can have lasting damaging effects on a little child.[16]

I remember the rude awakening I experienced when I graduated from high school and had to think about a job and college. Only then did I realize the security that I had as a child. Mom and Dad had taken care of everything—they worked, they paid the bills, they fed us and clothed us, and if there were problems in life, they took care of them. Every person should be able to grow up with this kind of love and security. But abuse shatters this world, bringing a sense of betrayal and vulnerability, causing incalculable damage.

While I have never experienced physical or sexual abuse and therefore can never truly know its pain or suffering, I've witnessed, in my wife Faith's life and in the lives of others I've come to know, the devastation it leaves behind.

While only the individual who has gone through abuse can truly know or feel what he or she is experiencing, it seems that a

---

16   Victoria L. Johnson, *Children and Sexual Abuse*, (Downers Grove, IL: Inter-Varsity Press, 2007), p, 7.

person who has suffered abuse goes through several stages in the healing process.

THE VICTIM STAGE

When someone has been raped or molested, the devastation is immense. When Faith shares her testimony, she recounts how not long after her dad began abusing her, in a sense she died emotionally. When victimization began, the world as she knew it fundamentally changed for the worse, without any certainty of what the future would hold. Pain, sadness, guilt, hatred, shame, fear, a loss of self-worth, and confusion all come flooding into the life. This only increased as the abuse continued.

Why did they become victims in the first place?

Many people wonder why the victimized one didn't do something to stop the abuse. Why didn't she cry out? Why didn't he run away?

But in all cases of sexual abuse, the offender has some sort of power over the victim. It can be age, strength, will, money, guilt, intimidation, threats, or any number of other things. Victims of sexual assault feel powerless to help themselves and powerless to escape their offender. "Children know they cannot withstand the attacks of adults who are always smarter and more powerful, so the only form of defense they know is acquiescence."[17] This is true of adult victims as well, who are groomed, manipulated, conditioned, threatened, and overpowered.[18]

---

17   Anderson, *When Child Abuse Comes to Church*, p. 39.

18   When Christians blame the victim, claiming that a woman "deserved" an assault because people say she dressed provocatively or acted flirty, when they

Why didn't the victims tell?

In almost all of our conferences and speaking engagements in churches, someone asks us, "Why don't victims report the abuse?" Pastor Bill Anderson said that in the case of widespread sexual abuse in his church, not one of the sixty victims reported the abuse.[19] There are many reasons why victims don't report their abuse, but two primary factors are fear and shame.

Child victims can be very confused by the lies told them by the offender. They can feel *shame* that they were actually at fault for the abuse. They can feel *fear* of the offender's many threats.[20]

Adult victims struggling with memories of abuse from the past fear that if they open their past, even a little bit, they'll never be able to recover from it, fear that they won't be believed, fear that they'll go through this potential re-traumatization without any good results, even fear of the unknown. They can also feel a deep sense of shame, even when the abuse very clearly was not their fault.

At a conference where we spoke, Faith and I heard a woman's story of sexual abuse. She told us that when she finally had the courage to tell her church, they immediately rejected her and refused to believe that her father would ever do something like that to her. She told us that the pain that she felt from this treatment by her church was like being raped all over again. "Believing that we have to remain

---

take a "Well, what was she expecting?" attitude, they show a calloused attitude of refusing to understand the criminal nature of sexual assault and the dynamics used to overpower the one under the control of the offender. This attitude is explored further in chapter 5, "Understand the Enablers."

19   Anderson, *When Child Abuse Comes to Church*, p. 55.

20   The offender's tactics are explored further in Chapter 3, "Understand the Offender."

silent about something confusing and painful that happened to us can be another form of victimization."[21]

Why do they keep struggling?

Sexual abuse carries with it a profound impact that those of us who have never been abused can find difficult to understand. This negative impact is affected by such factors as the age that the abuse began, the level of violence involved, the number of people that perpetrated abuse against the victim, and the length of time it continued.[22] Because of complicating factors such as dissociation and repression, the effects of the abuse can show up unexpectedly many years later.[23]

> Victims of sexual violation often report perverted sexual imaginations, such as fantasies of bondage or prostitution. These are deeply shameful and seem sinful. If you have these fantasies, you will certainly feel contaminated. However, these fantasies usually would not have existed without victimization. They are a tragic consequence of being linked to someone else's sin and violence.[24]

Because of the continuing fear, shame, and confusion, the lack of validation, and a sense of worthlessness, many victims have difficulty moving forward with their lives, often struggling

---

21   Wendy Maltz, *The Sexual Healing Journey* (New York: HarperCollins Publishers, 2012), p. 50.

22   Cameron Boyd, *The Impacts of Sexual Assault on Women* (Australian Institute of Family Studies, 2011), p. 1.

23   Chapter 4, "Face the Repercussions of the Sin," further explores the impact that sexual abuse continues to have on the life of an abuse victim.

24   Edward T. Welch, *Shame Interrupted: How God Lifts the Pain of Worthlessness and Rejection* (Greensboro, NC: New Growth Press, 2012), p. 16.

with jobs, relationships, sometimes with a sense of being unable to cope with life. [25]

A word of hope for victims

Someone has caused great harm to you, but God is bigger—He has taken you out of that abuse and brought you here.[26] Through the centuries, Christians have been comforted by the words in Hebrews 13:5-6, which say, "'I will never leave you nor forsake you.' So we may boldly say: 'The Lord is my helper; I will not fear. What can man do to me?'" This verse may cause some abuse victims to recoil because it seemed that God was absent in your abuse. But this scripture is not saying that people will never hurt those who trust in God—that has happened since the beginning of time. Rather, it's saying that none of the evil man can do will keep God from being faithful to His promises to those who trust Him. No harm that others can do will keep you from God or keep God from you. As you continue to look to Him, you'll see glimpses again and again that He has not forsaken you; man cannot harm you enough to force God's presence to abandon you. He is Immanuel, "God with us."[27]

Unlike the evil ones who perpetrated great harm, Jesus saw great value in little children, as He did in every soul, no matter how weak and helpless. He says in Matthew 18:10, "Take heed that you do not despise one of these little ones, for I say to you that in heaven their

---

25   An important factor in a continued sense of victimization is the work of enablers, explored further in Chapter 5, "Understand the Enablers."

26   If you are still in an abusive situation as you read this, we urge you to tell someone you can trust who can help you navigate the process of getting to safety. Chapters 10 and 12 give more detail about what church leaders and others can and should do to help you.

27   Matthew 1:23.

angels always see the face of my Father who is in heaven." Jesus gave a serious warning to anyone who "despises" a child, looking down on the child with contempt, or regarding the child as worthless.

Think about the picture that God paints in this verse: every child has an angel who is beholding God's face. The angel is protective of these precious children and stands before God the Father on behalf of every child. The implication is that if you harm this child, you will pay a severe price. If all of this will happen to someone who despises a child, what in the world do we think will happen to someone who rapes or molests a child? A day is coming when God will unleash His wrath upon this world and on those who practice evil, but in the meantime, Romans 2:5 says they are "treasuring up for [themselves] wrath in the day of wrath."

If you have gone through abuse, know that in spite of the evil deeds that evil people have perpetrated on you, God dearly loves you and wants to comfort you and bring healing into your life. God may use someone in your life right now to help bring comfort and hope. We're praying for you, that a friend or counselor you can trust will become evident to you in the midst of your woundedness.[28]

MOVING FROM VICTIM TO SURVIVOR

Though the distinction often isn't clear, a goal for people who have been sexually violated is to be able to move away from finding their identity as a victim. They consider themselves "survivors" when they're able to move on with life in spite of the pain and damage, able to hold a good job, or even establish a career. Their relationships are relatively stable, and they can get married and become loving parents.

---

28   See also Chapter 13, "The Abuse Survivor's Shepherd."

Though people in the victim stage struggle to stand, those whom we would call survivors have found a way to stand, maybe by reaching out to God or to a compassionate friend or wise counselor. Ecclesiastes 4:9–10 says, "Two are better than one . . . For if they fall, one will lift up his companion. But woe to him who is alone when he falls, for he has no one to help him up."

For the most part, survivors have had an opportunity to process their difficulties and pain, often through counseling, and come to terms with many aspects of what they've experienced.

More healing needed?

In the survivor stage, there is a measure of healing, but sometimes it can be like a person with cancer who can put on a good front but inside may still be in misery. To the world, and sometimes even to close friends, survivors for the most part look well and appear to have it all together, but for many, on the inside it can still be as though the assault happened yesterday with all the hurt and anger, the guilt and shame. As Heitritter and Vought have observed, "Many survivors of sexual abuse have tremendous anger toward God, their parents, and other Christians who did not understand the deep pain of the abuse they endured."[29]

If you listen to survivors tell their story and watch the tears come into their eyes or hear the pain, fear, shame, or anger that comes into their voices, you can recognize that the wounds are still not fully healed. My wife, Faith, was a survivor. Faith has great secretarial skills and is a kind and loving person, but her healing was only superficial.

---

29   Lynn Heitritter and Jeanette Vought, *Helping Victims of Sexual Abuse: A Sensitive Biblical Guide for Counselors, Victims, and Families* (Minneapolis: Bethany House Publishers, 2006), p. 67.

It wasn't until we started our ministry to speak out against sexual abuse and she came forward with her story in order to help others that a deeper level of healing began to take place.

As survivors continue on the healing journey, one of the most important choices they can make is the choice to replace lies with truth. The offender implanted vicious lies in the midst of trauma. The enablers have—wittingly or unwittingly—often reinforced and added more lies. Counselors who can help survivors effectively replace lies with truth without heaping on them any shame or guilt can be very beneficial in helping the survivor move from a place of sadness to a place of joy.[30]

BECOMING A VICTOR

The third stage in the life of a sexual abuse victim, the stage that we hope everyone will reach, is victory. As I was writing this book, I discovered that in Webster's dictionary the word *victor* immediately follows the word *victim*. Webster describes a victor as "one who defeats an enemy."

For those who have been assaulted, though the offender is an enemy and the memories may seem like enemies, the real enemy is the forces of darkness, because the most important battle we wage is the unseen one. A true victor is no longer held prisoner by hate, fear, shame, or a sense of guilt. Victors have moved from being victims who can't cope, to being survivors who have learned how to cope, to

---

30 Dealing with trauma—pain that has been short-circuited in processing— is another important factor in abuse healing. Counselors who understand the nature of trauma and have effective tools for dealing with it can serve as lifelines for abuse survivors. Ideally, our churches will form partnerships with such counselors. The website www.globaltraumarecovery.org gives much helpful information on this topic. See also Chapter 10, "What Our Churches Must Do."

completely breaking free from the prison that enslaved them. Being a victor doesn't mean that you don't still sometimes feel the pain or have memories that you struggle with. It means that you have faced your enemy and broken his grip over you.

Complete victory in anyone's life can be found only in Jesus Christ. In her excellent book *On the Threshold of Hope*, Dr. Diane Langberg discusses how healing for the survivor's body, emotions, thinking, relationships, and spirit, are all found in the Redeemer of the soul. Having counseled survivors of sexual abuse for over thirty years, Dr. Langberg says, "How has such a thing happened [as healing]? It has happened because there is a Redeemer. I know him, and I have seen his work. It is a good work, and he is faithful to it."[31]

Over the years as I've worked with abuse survivors who suffer from depression, self-doubt, and a sense of worthlessness, I've seen that one of the things that has been a great help to these people is, after dealing truthfully with their own issues, after receiving God's comfort, to then take opportunities to reach out and help others. For the thirty years of our marriage, having walked with Faith through the struggles she has experienced as a result of her abuse and on her healing journey in Christ, I believe that only since coming forward with her story in order to bring hope and comfort to others has she truly become a victor. Faith has healed and grown and flourished more in the past few years than in the previous two decades combined.

We read in 2 Corinthians 1:3–4, "Blessed be the God and Father of our Lord Jesus Christ, the Father of mercies and God of all comfort,

---

31   Diane Langberg, Ph.D., *On the Threshold of Hope: Opening the Door to Healing for Survivors of Sexual Abuse* (Carol Stream, Illinois: Tyndale House Publishers, Inc., 1999), p. 138.

who comforts us in all our tribulation, that we may be able to comfort those who are in any trouble, with the comfort with which we ourselves are comforted by God." Sexual abuse is a very serious matter that changes life for the abuse survivor forever. Through knowing and believing and speaking the truth, without fear and shame, an abuse victim can become a victor and can find joy in helping others as well.[32]

> *My pastor tells me that I am a casualty of war. Satan is fighting a war against God and used my abuser as a front-line fighter who attacked me. In the battle I was greatly injured by an agent of Satan, but God will ultimately destroy him. Now God has brought me away from all that to a safe place. My pastor said that even though this abuse was very big in my life, eventually it will fade into the background of who I am. It will always be a part of me, but it won't define me. The gaping wounds will heal and fade into battle scars that blend in and are overshadowed by what God is doing in my life. My pastor wants me to eventually counsel others. I'm not hopeless.[33]*

---

32   For more about the truth that must replace the lies, see Chapter 13, "The Abuse Survivor's Shepherd."

33   Personal correspondence, used by permission.

CHAPTER 3

UNDERSTAND THE OFFENDERS

Someone who rapes or molests another person not only causes incalculable pain and damage, but he[34] also breaks God's law as well as the law of the land. In our ignorance of the prevalence and complexities of the sin of sexual abuse, the twisted nature of offenders, and the innocent and "normal" appearance that offenders so often present, we thought that Faith was her father's only victim and had hoped and assumed that he had repented and was a changed person.

How wrong we were.

MASTER HYPOCRITES

Faith and I, married less than a year, sat in the pew listening to Faith's father as he preached. He hopped from church to church so much—preaching in one for six months, another for

---

34   Though we understand that approximately 3-5% of sexual offenders are women and we do personally know stories about women having seriously molested children, since the vast majority of offenders are men, we'll be using the male pronoun throughout this book, with the understanding that women offenders are included.

a year—that he could hardly be called a pastor. All he did was preach on Sunday. But that's what he was called.

"It's worldly," he shouted into the microphone. He was talking about contemporary Christian music again. Then he got off on the subject of smoking. "Why are you putting that tar in your lungs?" He pounded the pulpit. "Your body . . . is the temple . . . of the Holy . . . Spirit!" His tone became more condescending, more harsh, more sanctimonious, with each word.

I looked down at the verse in 1 Corinthians. You molested your daughter, and you're still preaching about your body being the temple of the Holy Spirit?

I didn't even know then about all the other children he had molested and the women he had seduced, some of them even in the church building itself.

In the 1993 movie *Dennis the Menace,* Christopher Lloyd plays Switchblade Sam, a disheveled, evil-looking man whom one might think to be the quintessential child molester. But the fact is that a child molester—or one who rapes adults—can look like a very ordinary person, even a good Christian.[35]

[A]busers can be rich or poor, smart or stupid, boorish or charming, failed or successful, black or white, or any other skin color, for that matter. Even some of the judges,

---

35   As examples of a criminal's ability to seem like "such a nice guy," consider the CIA spies Robert Hanssen and Aldrich Ames, who deceived fellow members of the CIA as "such nice guys" for decades while they sold intelligence information to Russia, causing the deaths of many of their compatriots. See http://www. crimelibrary.com/terrorists_spies/spies/ames/1.html.

prosecutors, police officers, and social workers whose job it is to put child molesters behind bars and to protect their victims, have been convicted of molesting children.[36]

Dr. Anna Salter, a psychologist who has interviewed hundreds of child molesters in prison, quotes one young man who had served as a deacon in his church and had molested ninety-five children in his youth groups:

> *I lived a double life. . . . I would do kind and generous things for people. I would give families money . . . from my own bank accounts. I would support them in all the ways that I could. Talk to them, encourage them. I would go to nursing homes. Talk with the elderly. Pray with the elderly. I would do community service projects. Pick up litter off the side of the road. I would mow the lawns for elderly and handicapped people. Go grocery shopping for them. . . . They immediately rallied to my defense when I was accused of being a sexual offender. They said, "We know this young man. He has been in our community all of his life. . . . This is not something that he would do. This is not something that goes along with behavior that we see him in day in and day out," and that was true because I was very careful that they did not see that behavior day in and day out.[37]*

The fact is that though churches don't necessarily breed predators (although that can be the case), predators often seek out certain

---

36   John Crewdson, *By Silence Betrayed: Sexual Abuse of Children in America* (Boston: Little, Brown and Company, 1988), p. 55.

37   Anna C. Salter, Ph. D., *Predators: Pedophiles, Rapists, and Other Sex Offenders* (New York: Basic Books, 2003), p. 31.

kinds of churches where they can fit quite nicely. Voyle Glover offers some reasons:

1. Little or no screening of workers

2. The tendency to see only good in people

3. Uncritical acceptance of a person's confession of faith

4. Lots and lots of children

5. Frequent unfettered access to children

6. Lack of monitoring

7. Untrained workers and staff

8. The tendency to cover or minimize a crime[38]

These observations boil down to naïve trust and thinking the best of people—especially volunteer workers!—who are within the ministry. This trust creates the perfect environment for sexual offenders. A good church-going, ministry-participating man is hardly likely to be suspected of being a child molester, rapist, or abuser. One abuse survivor wrote:

> As soon as he graduated from [a certain Christian university], my abuser joined the Baptist church I attended and became my elementary classroom teacher in my Christian school. He was jovial and well liked. No one questioned him going to get bulletin board materials or having a student help him. There was always a good reason for him to be in that out-of-the-way storage room with me. By the time I figured out some sort of name for what he did

---

38   Voyle Glover, *Protecting Your Church Against Sexual Predators* (Grand Rapids: Kregel Publications, 2005), p. 36.

to me I didn't dare tell, because I was sure I would be labeled as the school whore.[39]

In Guinea, West Africa, the Mamou Alliance Academy was an out-of-the-way missionary boarding school where terrible abuse took place. To most Christians, this school would outwardly appear to be the model missionary school—every day the children sat in chapel singing and memorizing verses. But what was happening in secret was vile indeed. One lady in our church attended this boarding school as a child and witnessed the rampant sexual and physical abuse perpetrated by some of the missionaries who were supposed to care for the children. The film *All God's Children* recounts stories of this abuse.[40] I watched it with tears as I listened to the survivors describing how they were told to sing hymns and memorize verses by the same ones who at night were raping, molesting, and beating them. One abuse survivor said that for years whenever she would think of God she would see only the face of her offender. These religious offenders are like the Pharisees of Jesus' day to whom Jesus said in Matthew 23:27, "Woe to you, scribes and Pharisees, hypocrites! For you are like white-washed tombs which indeed appear beautiful outwardly, but inside are full of dead men's bones and all uncleanness."

---

39   Personal correspondence, used by permission.

40   This video is available for free viewing on YouTube or can be purchased from www.allgodschildrenthefilm.com. Wes Stafford, former president of Compassion International, who also spent part of his childhood at Mamou, describes some of the abuse in his book *Too Small to Ignore: Why the Least of These Matters Most*, in the chapter tellingly titled "Breaking the Silence" (Colorado Springs: Waterbrook Press, 2007), p. 143-159.

SKILLFUL OPPORTUNISTS

When offenders are caught, some people may excuse their behavior by claiming that they had a mental illness. But "one myth about sex abusers is that they are insane. . . . They know what they are doing is wrong. That is why they go to such lengths to keep it secret."[41]

The problem was it was such a big secret, everything was such a big secret in my family. No one talked about anything. Everything about our lives when I was growing up, it was a secret.[42]

In actuality, when offenders make a practice of raping and molesting, they develop "skills" that help them go from one victim to another without getting caught.

When a person like myself wants to obtain access to a child, you don't just go up and get the child and sexually molest the child. There's a process of obtaining the child's friendship and, in my case, also obtaining the family's friendship and their trust. When you get their trust, that's when the child becomes vulnerable and you can molest the child.[43]

Not only do offenders have evil intent, but many of them can and do strike so quickly that no one would think it would be possible that something that bad could happen in such a short time. In his book *The Serpents Among Us,* Patrick Crough recounts one of the cases

---

41   Anderson, *When Child Abuse Comes to Church,* pp. 52-53.

42   Abuse survivor quoted in Ann W. Annis, Michelle Loyd-Paige, Rodger R. Rice, *Set Us Free: What the Church Needs to Know from Survivors of Abuse* (New York: Calvin College Social Research Center and University Press of America, Inc., 2001), p. 60.

43   Salter, *Predators,* p. 42.

he worked on in which an offender needed only minutes with two children to do the unthinkable.

> Within a twenty-minute time frame, [this offender] sexually assaulted one little girl in front of another and even brazenly memorialized the event on camera, while one of their mothers was right upstairs visiting with two other women.[44]

Besides the many stories of incest we've heard, we also hear stories of single moms with boyfriends. For a pedophile (an offender who is attracted only to children) a single mother with young children can be an ideal scenario. The single mom is usually very needy, and the children need a father figure. The sexual predator will use this relationship to get access to the children. In many cases the mom is working, and the boyfriend has complete control of the children while she is gone, so that the children become trapped in their own home. Adults who were sex trafficked as children have told us that they lived two lives—the normal life of going to school and church, and the dark, secret life of sex trafficking, often at the hands of a father or stepfather or mother's boyfriend.[45]

DEVIOUS MANIPULATORS

Faith's growing-up years were a nightmare. Behind the four walls of their house, their father would scream and yell, physically abusing her brothers and emotionally abusing her mother. He created chaos

44   Patrick Crough, *The Serpents Among Us: How to Protect Your Children from Sexual Predators—A Police Investigator's Perspective* (Millstone Justice, 2009), p. 184.

45   Jerome Elam is a former sex trafficking victim who blogs poignantly about the double life of his childhood, for example in "The story of one. Trafficked Boys: Vandalized innocence hidden in plain sight," *Communities Digital News*, September 20, 2014.

and fear in the home, often threatening suicide, in order to beat the family into submission. For Faith, when her dad began raping and molesting her, she felt as if she had nowhere to turn.

Perpetrators of sexual assault are skilled manipulators, assuring the silence of their victims through a variety of tricks and lies that always come back to the element of power that they hold over the victims. If they couldn't succeed in keeping their victims silent, they wouldn't be able to continue to perpetrate their evil crimes.

One way offenders keep victims silent is through threats— threats of loss of family, ministry, or even life. One woman who shared her story told us that in her presence, her father put a gun to her brother's head and told her that if she ever told anyone about his abuse of her that he would kill her brother and mother and then kill himself, leaving only her alive, to bear the burden that all these deaths would be her fault.

Another method of manipulation is through forced "forgiveness." The woman who was abused by her elementary school teacher wrote:

> [The sexual abuse] depended on how I wore my hair, what type of clothes I wore (jumpers infuriated him), and whether or not it was what he wanted. If I ran from him, wasn't where he sent me when he arrived, fought too much or not enough; then what happened [the raping and molesting] was my fault. . . . When I refused to forgive him, I would lose the 45-minute recess and have to stand at the wall. He would stand next to me as I faced the wall doing my time during recess, and tell me I knew what I had to do to get off the wall. How could a man quote so many Bible verses to prove his point and guilt a child into proving she really forgave him day

after day, week after week for a whole school year and each and every time molest or rape her again?[46]

Offenders on the mission field, such as in the case of Mamou Alliance Academy, threatened their child victims with eternal punishment—not just for the victims, but for the *Africans.* "If you tell, your parents will have to leave the mission field, and then Africans will go to hell."[47] The children loved the Africans and didn't want to be the cause of the ones they loved suffering eternal punishment. So they themselves suffered in silence.

Offenders can groom their victims by flattering them, buying them things, or doing something special for them. They can work at developing a relationship of dependence in which the victim believes that she has to keep the secret to protect her abuser.

As a young woman, and even younger in the faith, I became part of a thriving youth ministry as a staff member. I identified with my boss, a pastor, 18 years my senior, as sort of a father figure. I became emotionally attached to him, and then he groomed me for a sexual encounter—and blamed me. . . . He seemed stronger, a leader, confident, able to direct things. . . . After each physical interaction, he would comfort me and blame me at the same time, yet appear to everyone else as this amazing, caring, pastor who wanted what was best for everyone. Very skilled at image management. . . . The pattern between us became one of crisis: me not knowing what to do and going to him for help. Most of the time, he would intentionally stir up pain in me (talking about my mom or other painful things

---

46   Personal correspondence, used by permission.

47   *All God's Children,* DVD, 2008, www.allgodschildrenthefilm.com.

that I had disclosed to him). I would get to a place of absolute emotional despair; he would move in on me physically, increasing my despondency over "what I had done." Then he would be the "comforter." My abuser was my friend in order to abuse.[48]

Another way that sexual perpetrators keep their victims in subjection is to tell them that they are worthless, no one loves them, and this is happening to them because they are bad. They will blame them for the abuse—it was the way that they dressed or the way that they acted. One woman told us how her abuser sneered "whore" every time he abused her. Another woman told us that after years of sexual abuse by her father, she felt so filthy that she actually thought others could smell the stench she gave off. Another told us that she believed she could never, ever get clean no matter how hard she tried. Precious children, and even young adults, are also being beaten, both verbally and physically, into submission. They are being constantly deceived in order that evil people can have their own gratification.

HAVING A SEARED CONSCIENCE

The deacons shifted in their seats, uncomfortable. It was November of 2005, and they sat together in a meeting with Faith's father, who had just been found as having molested not only his foster granddaughter, but a number of other girls. They had never faced a problem like this before.

"If you're truly repentant," they said, "and you bring forth fruits of repentance, maybe you can eventually return to ministry. You

---

48   Erik Campano, "Presbyterian Pastor Doubles as Escort: CSBV III," www. patheos.com, May 24, 2013. The woman telling her story in this article is a personal friend.

won't be able to minister to women and children again, but you might be able to have a ministry with men."

He raised his eyebrows, quizzical. "I'm not ready to be a homosexual," he said.

When I first heard that, I rolled my eyes, thinking he just wanted to make every statement into a sexual statement.

But then I realized that it was much more. It was a revelation of his thought processes.

"I'm not ready to be a homosexual" meant that his entire so-called ministry was oriented around sex.

"I'm not ready to be a homosexual" meant that the purpose of his ministry was to gain access to victims.

Ministry was about having sex with girls, not preaching the gospel. It was about himself, not others; it was about sin, not righteousness. Ministry meant having a steady stream of potential victims, nothing more.

Two weeks after confessing the deed, he was in another church, singing in the choir. His conscience didn't trouble him at all.

"Death ain't no big deal," he sang in church. "Let me tell you, death ain't no big deal." Always confident, always smug. There was no sin problem for him.

But he has never once shown true repentance of any of his crimes. I believe that when he has to account for his deeds before the Judge of all the earth, he'll find that death will be a very big deal for him.

How can they harm other people this way? It's a natural question. How can they purposely cause such excessive devastation? Studies have been conducted trying to understand why most sexual offenders seem to be untroubled by that nagging thing most of us experience called a conscience.[49]

One study found that child molesters average 49 victims and 114 acts of molestation.[50] In another study, 23 rapists and 30 child molesters were interviewed with a guarantee of confidentiality. The following results were found: The 23 rapists had been arrested 43 times, but they admitted to 5,090 sex crimes total, including 319 child molestations and 178 rapes. The 30 child molesters had been arrested 45 times, but they admitted to more than 20,000 sex offenses, including nearly 6,000 child molestations and 213 rapes. This means that from 53 men there were 17,000 victims.[51]

Staggering statistics. We can only imagine how easy it is for one offender, untroubled by conscience, to destroy a whole family, a church, or a community.[52]

---

49   In *The Sociopath Next Door* (New York: Three Rivers, 2005), author Martha Stout argues for the absence of conscience. The Bible speaks of a "searing" or "hardening" of conscience, a lack of empathy that is verified in psychological research about sociopaths.

50   Referenced in The Abel and Harlow Child Molestation Prevention Study, excerpted from Gene G. Abel, M.D., and Nora Harlow, *The Stop Child Molestation Book* (Xlibris, 2001), accessed via http://www.childmolestationprevention.org/pdfs/study.pdf.

51   Freeman-Longo study cited in Anna C. Salter, Ph.D., *Transforming Trauma: A Guide to Understanding and Treating Adult Survivors* (New York: Sage Publications, Inc., 1995), p. 9.

52   Studies like these draw a clear distinction between the two types of child molesters: pedophiles and non-pedophiles. Pedophiles, who are attracted to children who have not yet begun to develop as adults, molest up to ten times as many children as non-pedophiles.

Though a book of this nature won't go into details about abuse, it's important for the Christian world to recognize that abusers are not known for their gentleness. We've heard stories of secret abuse by "good church people" that we would never have thought would happen among those who claim the name of Christ. Bill Anderson, in his book *When Child Abuse Comes to Church,* gives a more or less blow-by-blow account of his own church's discovery of and dealing with the sexual abuse that had been perpetrated by a church member—a teenage boy.

> In May 1990 as a result of increased pressure from his probation officer, Donald admitted further crimes against three of our children whom he had previously confessed to molesting. These disclosures were so gross that his therapist left the room and vomited in the hall.[53]

We also have heard stories so lurid that they have made us feel sick to our stomachs. Be assured that many of the crimes we're talking about, even among "good church people," are perverse and even violent crimes.

INSTINCTIVE BLAMERS, MINIMIZERS, AND SELF-DEFENDERS

"I'm like Job with his miserable comforters."

Faith's dad was telling the tractor story again. When he had been injured by a tractor, someone asked him what God was trying to teach him, what he was doing wrong. I know that isn't a very helpful question to ask a man when he's lying in a hospital bed, but it would have been good if my father-in-law had even once asked himself—or God—to show him what he was doing wrong.

---

53   Anderson, *When Child Abuse Comes to Church,* p. 104.

But no, he was just like Job, a poor, suffering Christian. And he told the tractor story over and over.

This time though, there was a special flavor to it.

This time he had been accused of molesting an underage girl—another one, before the one he admitted to. Somehow he convinced the family to drop the charges, and after they did, he went on and on about how judgmental people were, how mean people were, how he was being persecuted. The whine in his voice grated on my ears.

In 1 Samuel 15, God commanded King Saul to destroy all the inhabitants and animals of Amalek, but Saul chose to disobey. When Samuel confronted him with his disobedience, Saul's first response was denial: "But I have obeyed the voice of Lord, and gone on the mission on which the Lord sent me." When Samuel indicated to Saul that he knew he had done wrong, Saul chose to excuse the sin by blaming others: "The people took of the plunder, sheep and oxen." Saul's triple sin of disobedience, excusing, and blaming was not taken lightly. The kingdom was removed from him.

When God confronted Adam with his sin of eating the forbidden fruit, Adam blamed Eve and even blamed God for what he had done. "The *woman* whom *you* gave to be with me, *she* gave me and I ate." Many offenders who claim to be Christians will blame God for their vile behavior. They'll say, "God made me do this," or "God gave me these desires."

Another offender we know about admitted to molesting a young teenager. At a meeting with church elders, he said that she was "a troubled girl," claiming that she had seduced him. After criticizing his victim, he began criticizing her mother. It was a classic attempt to make everyone else look bad in an effort to make what he had done look less evil.

Another offender in a highly publicized case was a well-to-do man who served as a deacon in his church. After twice raping his family's babysitter, he minimized his sin as "unfaithfulness to his wife," with no mention of his dual rape of an underage girl.[54]

I entered the house with Faith's two brothers, one of them the foster father of the teenage girl Faith's dad had admitted to molesting. Dad had already called his son and acknowledged it, but of course it was the fourteen-year-old girl's fault. "Her hormones were racing out of control."

When we walked in, we saw him sitting on the couch, his hand on the open Bible beside him. Poised, as if playing a part in a drama.

"You know, God has been teaching me so much," he began. "I've been reading the Bible a lot—"

I steeled myself, cutting him off to take control of the meeting I had called. We prayed and then confronted him with his sin.

"I'm right with God." Tears began to come into his eyes. It was so easy for him to manufacture those.

I knew how I was supposed to interpret this scene: "You don't have to be involved anymore. You don't need to report anything to the authorities. Everything is taken care of."

---

54   "New Hampshire Man Found Guilty of Rape of Tina Anderson," ABC News, May 27, 2011, accessed at http://abcnews.go.com/2020/new-hampshire-man-ernest-willis-found-guilty-rape-tina-anderson/story?id=13702833.

We told him that if he was truly repentant, he needed to turn himself in the next day. Instead, he got an attorney.

We called the police.

"I'm just being persecuted," he blubbered, "like Job."

A FEW WARNING SIGNS

Based on his many years of experience with investigating sex abuse cases, Patrick Crough put together a list of warning signs that someone may be getting too close to your children. Though this is an incomplete list—and no point by itself means the person is grooming the child— it can provide a crucial starting point for parents, church leaders, and others who care.

1. Offers of assistance

2. Great personal investment

3. Seeking constant contact

4. Professionals seeking alone time with your child outside of their normal role

5. Teenage boys providing child care

6. Men making your life very convenient

7. Possessiveness

8. Solo travel

9. Interest in pornography

10. Excessive compliments[55]

---

55   Crough, *The Serpents Among Us*, pp. 301-303. Though Crough focuses on men who abuse, we acknowledge that at least 3-5% of offenders are women.

WHAT GOD SAYS ABOUT SEXUAL
ABUSE OFFENDERS

God's Word is very clear that if a believer sins, God will chasten him. First Corinthians 11 indicates that God would chastise an unrepentant believer even to the point of death. Hebrews 12:8 says, "But if you are without chastening, of which all have become partakers, then you are illegitimate and not sons." If someone who claims to be a Christian lives in a pattern of sin and never experiences the chastening of God, never experiences true repentance and remorse, then that is evidence that he is not really a Christian at all, that God does not dwell in him. First John 3:6 says, "Whoever abides in him does not sin [live in a pattern of sin]. Whoever sins [lives in a pattern of sin] has neither seen him nor known him."

So who are these unrepentant, unchastised unbelievers in our churches who claim to be Christians? In Jude 1:4 we read, "For certain men have crept in [to the churches] unnoticed, who long ago were marked out for this condemnation, ungodly men, who turn the grace of our God into lewdness and deny the only Lord God and our Lord Jesus Christ." Why does Jude refer to these men as sneaking in unnoticed? The text says that they were planning to commit immorality and knew certain Christians would be an easy target, because of the wrong teachings on grace.[56]

How easy it is to appear righteous when the church system stresses outward appearance and certain religious activities as the evidence of holiness! This is one of the surest ways to allow the creepers into your church. In Matthew 23:28 Jesus said to a similar

---

56   The misapplication of grace is addressed in Chapter 9, "Believe and Speak the Truth about Mercy and Justice, Grace and Love."

group who emphasized outward standards, "Even so you also out-wardly appear righteous to men, but inside you are full of hypocrisy and lawlessness."

"Beware of false prophets," Jesus warned his disciples, "who come to you in sheep's clothing, but inwardly they are ravenous wolves. You will know them by their fruits. Do men gather grapes from thornbushes or figs from thistles? Even so, every good tree bears good fruit, but a bad tree bears bad fruit. A good tree cannot bear bad fruit, nor can a bad tree bear good fruit. Every tree that does not bear good fruit is cut down and thrown into the fire. Therefore by their fruits you will know them."[57] The fruit of the sexual offender is a fruit that is produced in secret. But it will come out. Listen. Pay attention to the people who are speaking about the fruit produced in secret.

"Either make the tree good and its fruit good, or else make the tree bad and its fruit bad; for a tree is known by its fruit," Jesus castigated the Pharisees of his own day. "Brood of vipers! How can you, being evil, speak good things? For out of the abundance of the heart the mouth speaks. A good man out of the good treasure of his heart brings forth good things, and an evil man out of the evil treasure [of his heart] brings forth evil things."[58] Sexual offenders, in positions of deacon, Sunday school teacher, choir member, or even pastor, want us to believe that they are good Christians, right with God—and yet they produce the evil fruit of abuse. If the fruit is evil, then that

---

57   Matthew 7:15–20.
58   Matthew 12:33–35.

means the heart is evil, and the person is evil, like a poisonous viper in the congregation of the Lord.[59]

These offenders rape and molest over and over again because they are evil in their hearts. Too many Christians are naïve, thinking that offenders are really nice people who have just made a few mistakes. There is no excuse for this kind of thinking: people whose hearts have not been transformed by the power of the Holy Spirit do evil things because their hearts are evil. God hates sin and does not excuse it or look the other way.

After all, as a wise person has observed, "good people don't pretend to be bad, but bad people pretend to be good all the time."[60]

---

59   Some abuse survivors have been led to believe that their flashback, nightmares, depression, and other symptoms of PTSD are evil fruit of an evil heart. This is untrue, and is not what these Scriptures are referring to. Trauma reactions are not evil; they are natural, just as a racing heart is a natural response to a loud scream. Sexual abuse, on the other hand, is evil, and is the very kind of evil fruit these Scriptures are talking about.

60   Jeff Crippen, author of *A Cry for Justice*, in personal correspondence, used by permission.

CHAPTER 4

FACE THE REPERCUSSIONS OF THE SIN

The book of Nehemiah begins in sadness. Nehemiah, a Jewish slave in Persian captivity, had just learned about the devastation in his homeland. "So it was," he said, "when I heard these words, that I sat down and wept, and mourned for many days; I was fasting and praying before the God of heaven."[61] Nehemiah's appropriate response to the news of the devastation of his homeland was shock and grief. He was immobilized and prostrated by the news.

When he was able to return to his homeland, the first thing Nehemiah did was to survey the damage. From this survey he was able to determine that the distress he and his people were in was great.

When any catastrophe happens, like an earthquake or a tsunami, shock and grief are appropriate reactions. But surveyors in the helicopter can get an even greater grasp of the devastation that the natural disaster has wreaked, the broken homes, the destruction. They can see firsthand that the distress their community is in is great.

---

61   Nehemiah 1:4.

That's what this chapter is about.

The consequences of abuse begin in the life of the abuse survivor and spread out like shock waves from an earthquake, carrying havoc and destruction as they go. Statistics can count the individuals who have been abused, but they can't begin to give a total picture of the disaster. Though offenders often seem little concerned with the devastation, the husband or wife who marries an abuse survivor, the children of the abuse survivor, the friend who walks with an abuse survivor in the healing journey, and those who counsel the abuse survivor will all enter into that world and truly get a close-up look at the damage offenders have caused.

REPERCUSSIONS FOR THE ABUSE SURVIVOR

Research into the long-range, far-reaching impact of sexual abuse is fairly new, beginning only in about the 1970s.[62] Before that time, society in general thought (and many still think) that if damage can't be scientifically observed, then it isn't real, but all in the victim's head. However, many studies in the past forty years have shown over and over that the trauma and pain caused by sexual abuse—even in cases where there are no physical scars—needs to be taken very seriously.

Recently a group of pastors were sharing some of the difficult situations they faced in the ministry. Each one told horrific stories of young people hooked on drugs and alcohol, immorality, and forms of

---

62   It is only after acknowledging that a phenomenon exists that one can begin to study it. Victor Vieth, et al, observe that it was only in the 1970s that mandated reporting laws for child abuse finally came to include child sexual abuse. In the 1980s many new cases of child sexual abuse were brought to court, but skepticism that the allegations could possibly be true abounded in the academic and professional community and literature for at least another ten years. See Victor I. Vieth, Bette L. Bottoms, and Alison Perona, *Ending Child Abuse: New Efforts in Prevention, Investigation, and Training* (London: Routledge, 2005), pp. 8ff.

self-mutilation. It was sobering to realize that in each of these cases, there had been abuse by someone from their family or church.

I love to hike, but twice during my teenage years I became lost in the woods. I still remember the feeling when I realized I wasn't going in the right direction. I felt disoriented and almost dizzy, frustrated and directionless. It's the same with abuse survivors. People who have been abused often lose their moral compass. They become confused and disoriented about life and have trouble determining what is right and wrong. What they knew inside to be wrong, their offender told them was okay. When they sensed themselves to be a victim, their offender told them it was their own fault. This is especially true when the offender was supposed to be a spiritual protector or role model—everything in the abuse survivor's life has been turned upside down.

Shattering of love

Love is a beautiful and positive emotion that brings warmth, security, happiness, and a sense of well-being. But when a person has been sexually assaulted by a parent or someone else in a position of power or authority, it shatters the true meaning of love. This confusion carries into the adult life, where an abuse survivor may find it very difficult to love or to accept love in its true form.

Confusion and fear

Confusion and fear can reign in the mind of sexual assault victims who have been told "No one will believe you" or "It's really all your fault" or "Good children always obey" or "When you say 'no,' it really means 'yes'" or "You're so filthy now that God would never accept you," or any of hundreds of other lies that offenders have whispered in their ears. Far from the old saying, "Words will never hurt me," Proverbs 18:21 tells us, "Death and life are in the power of the tongue." Throughout their lives, even without their realizing it, the lies that abusers have told the victims can shout far louder than the truth of God's love for them.[63]

Heitritter and Vought describe how abuse impacted the life of one victim. "The guilt, shame, and confusion were indescribable and agonizing. Didn't God care about her? . . . She became very angry with God. . . ."[64]

Each week we receive new reports from people who were harmed by this sin. One such report was from a woman who, as a nine-year-old pastor's daughter, was raped by a guest speaker who was staying in their home. He threatened that if she told anyone, terrible things would happen to her parents and her father would have to leave the ministry, so she kept the secret. The next morning this man spoke in their church as though nothing had happened. For years this woman thought she would go to hell because of what the abuser had done to her.

People who have been sexually violated can also suffer confusion about proper boundaries in their lives. As Cloud and Townsend point out in their book *Boundaries*, the skin is the most basic boundary of all, and victims of sexual abuse have been fed the lie that "their property did not really begin at their skin. Others could invade their

---

63   The Truth to combat the lies is presented more fully in Chapter 13, "The Abuse Survivor's Shepherd."

64   Heitritter and Vought, *Helping Victims of Sexual Abuse*, p. 61.

property and do whatever they wanted."[65] As a result, "victims often feel that they are public property—that their resources, body, and time should be available to others just for the asking."[66]

> *I can't even remember the boys' faces. All I knew was that someone wanted something from me, and I felt it was my duty to give it to them—for no other reason than that they wanted it! I felt that I had no say-so in the matter.*[67]

Shame

Shame, a profound sense of disgrace and guilt that leads to self-hatred, will descend on victims who believe they were at fault for the abuse—a trick used by many offenders. "[E]veryone experiences shame to some degree. But sexually abused people often feel marked for life. The exposure of the past abuse sets them apart from normal, supposedly unstained, undamaged people."[68] One abuse survivor shared with us that as a young child she was raped and molested for many years by her father. In her heart-wrenching story, she tried to describe her feelings of guilt and pain and how she thought others would think that she was dirty. This sense was so strong that she thought she gave off a foul odor. "Shame is a response to helplessness, the violation of bodily integrity, and the indignity suffered in the

---

65   Dr. Henry Cloud and Dr. John Townsend, *Boundaries: When to Say Yes How to Say No to Take Control of Your Life* (Grand Rapids: Zondervan, 2002), p. 36.

66   Ibid., p. 234.

67   Ibid., p. 282.

68   Dr. Dan B. Allender, *The Wounded Heart: Hope for Adult Victims of Childhood Sexual Abuse* (Colorado Springs: NavPress, 2008), p. 63.

eyes of another person."[69] How sad for children to be so harmed, that they bear the shame and guilt for what has been done to them, while the offenders go on with their lives as though nothing were wrong. As Dr. Ed Welch says in *Shame Interrupted,* "When sex happens outside its intended boundaries, it brings shame on the victim. It *should* bring shame on the perpetrator."[70]

Shattered trust

Shattered trust occurs when one who was supposed to care for you has violated you instead. One woman who came to us shared that as a young lady she had gone to a pastor for help and counseling, but each time she went, he molested her. Her trust was broken, and to this day she bears the scars of spiritual wounding.

Especially if a non-offending parent fails to help and try to protect the victim, the victim's trust will be broken. In many cases, victims fear that if they go to authorities—their school or church authorities, or even the police—they still won't be protected. Too many stories have played out exactly this way for us to be able to give confident assurance otherwise. The entire sense of security that is so vital for living a normal life is now gone—it has been completely shattered.

Traumatic disorders

Traumatic disorders also often result. Dr. Philip G. Monroe and Dr. Diane Langberg, the founders of Global Trauma Recovery Institute (GTRI), include sexual abuse as one very significant type of trauma. Though with the news of soldiers developing PTSD

---

69   Judith Lewis Herman, *Trauma and Recovery: The Aftermath of Violence—from Domestic Abuse to Political Terror* (Basic Books, 1997), p. 53.

70   Welch, *Shame Interrupted, p. 14.*

(post-traumatic stress disorder) symptoms, people may believe that they understand what trauma is, many still don't recognize the symptoms of trauma or understand how to treat them. Trauma is defined by GTRI as "Exposure to a terrifying event which threatens life, bodily or psychological integrity and which evokes feelings of helplessness, overwhelming normal ways of coping. The experience results in repeating patterns of re-experiencing and/or avoiding the memory; anxiety and increased arousal as well as challenges to a person's sense of self, faith and future."[71] Clinical psychologist Dr. Jim Wilder, developer of the THRIVE training program, defines trauma this way:

> Trauma is damage caused by an impactful event that negatively alters our identity, integrity or function. While trauma has traditionally been defined by the size of an event needed to damage an average person, we define trauma as *the damage done when the impact of an event exceeds a person's capacity at that moment.*[72] (Italics added.)

Cloud and Townsend, in *Boundaries*, use the metaphor of a growing tree. Certain problems can happen such as the tree failing to receive enough nutrients, water, or sun. But trauma, they say, "is like lightning hitting the tree."[73]

Trauma responses are very natural in the body's and soul's reactions to sexual abuse. These include substance abuse, depression,

---

71   www.globaltraumarecovery.org/what-is-trauma/.

72   E. James Wilder, Edward M. Khouri, Chris M. Coursey, and Shelia D. Sutton, *Joy Starts Here: the transformation zone* (East Peoria, IL: Shepherd's House Inc., 2013), p. 245.

73   Cloud and Townsend, *Boundaries, pp. 82-83.*

chronic anxiety, chronic medical conditions, and compulsive behaviors such as excessive exercise[74] and eating disorders.[75] Eating disorders include anorexia, compulsive eating, and bulimia, which have been connected with sexual abuse in as many as 35-55% of cases studied.[76] Abuse also often propels a victim to self-mutilation born out of the agony and desperation. Because of the effects of the trauma on the brain, abuse victims can suffer from flashbacks (suddenly feeling "in" the traumatic situation), somatic symptoms ("body memories" such as smelling the same smell or feeling the same pain), emotional numbing, and dissociation.[77]

Struggles with faith

Struggles with faith in God can result in the life of a sexual assault victim, especially one who repeatedly asked for God's deliverance from the evil offender and felt as if God was silent, cold, and distant. Unless survivors have compassionate people in their lives to walk with them on the sometimes long road of healing, assuring

---

74   Maltz, *The Sexual Healing Journey*, p. xix.

75   Jacqueline M. Hirth, Mahbubur Rahman, and Abbey B. Berenson, *Journal of Women's Health*. August 2011, 20(8): 1141-1149. doi:10.1089/jwh.2010.2675.

76   Striegel-Moore RH, Dohm FA, Pike KM, Wilfley DE, Fairburn CG. "Abuse, bullying, and discrimination as risk factors for binge eating disorder," *American Journal of Psychiatry*, 2002 Nov; 159(11):1902-7.

77   Dissociation is a coping mechanism that, at the time of the trauma, can be essential in helping the victim, especially a child, to endure it. Though dissociation can take different forms, two of the major ones are "going away," a sense of being separated from the traumatic event, even sometimes into an imaginary world; and "splitting," in which the victim is able to create different identities to endure the trauma, so that the primary identity can live a more or less normal life. If the trauma wounds aren't eventually healed, the dissociation that served as a lifesaver during childhood trauma can become a crippling hindrance to living a normal life as an adult. For more information, see http://www.nami.org/Content/NavigationMenu/Inform_Yourself/About_Mental_Illness/By_Illness/Dissociative_Identity_Disorder.htm.

them of love without trying to offer pat answers, survivors may abandon faith altogether.[78]

If you have been hit by a drunk driver and are now in the hospital with multiple broken bones and internal injuries, you can forgive the driver that hit you, but the forgiveness process will not heal your injuries. You need medical care and time for your wounds to heal. Some injuries may leave permanent damage that can never be repaired outside of a miracle from God's hand. The same is true for the emotional and spiritual injuries that are suffered by ones who have been sexually abused. They can forgive their offenders, but their injuries will still take time to heal, and some wounds may be permanent.

Just as an infected wound that has scabbed over will need to be cut open in order to save the person's life, traumatic memories that have been stuffed away in a corner of the mind must be brought out and dealt with in order for the abuse survivor to find full healing. Counselors trained in trauma therapy as well as compassionate family and friends can form an important part of the support team to help the abuse survivor on the road to full recovery.

A letter to church people from an abuse survivor

In trying to explain how an abuse survivor can feel regarding the trauma and the shame, one abuse survivor wrote a very graphic description.

> It feels as if I got a very serious burn in a very private area. Each person comes in and has to open the bandage to see the damage. It isn't enough to try to describe it in words. They each want to see.

---

78   See Chapter 12, "How Family and Friends Must Help."

So, again and again, I endure the humiliation . . . (not done yet) so because of the infection, the smell is horrific and feels like part of me. Each time the bandage is lifted, the stench fills the room.

People can't help but have a look of horror from the smell and sight. Some turn away in disgust. Some seem too interested. When it seems it couldn't be any worse, I realize that I don't even have control of my bowels and they are watching me [soil] myself. Humiliation upon humiliation.

Then they have to talk to others and find out their view and description of my wounds, the stench, the [soiling], etc. They ask those who have compassion, but they also ask the ones who view me with disgust and want me to appear disgusting. So they talk to the people who describe the smell of my [excrement], the disgust of the smells, how I deserved the wound, how gross and defiled I am. I wonder at the end how anyone could see me as anything good. They have all seen the filth—the worst of it.

How can they ever look at my face again and not be overwhelmed by the memories of what they saw? The wounds eating away at my flesh, the filthy smelly rot that they gag on. That is me. I feel like they are watching me [soil myself] all over the place. Everyone just watches.

I read one time, that in some country, after raping the women, they cut them so their bowels will always leak so the victim will always be an outcast—smelly and separated from everyone. That is what I feel like.[79]

---

79   Personal correspondence, used by permission.

REPERCUSSIONS FOR THE
MARRIAGE AND FAMILY

The horrors of abuse and its memories kill intimacy—which in turn can destroy a marriage. As a pastor, I have seen many broken relationships in which abuse played a role in the struggles.[80]

When I told a young man about our Speaking Truth in Love Ministries, he immediately began telling me about the problems with intimacy in his marriage because of the abuse in his wife's past. Meaningful intimacy is vital for a healthy marriage, something beautiful that God made to be fully enjoyed by the husband and wife. There is a reason that the Holy Spirit inspired Paul to write to the believers at Corinth with this careful guidance for complete mutuality in the marriage relationship. In 1 Corinthians 7:3–5, he says, "Let the husband render to his wife the affection due her, and likewise also the wife to her husband. The wife does not have authority over her own body, but the husband does. And likewise the husband does not have authority over his own body, but the wife does. Do not deprive one another except with consent for a time, that you may give yourselves to fasting and prayer; and come together again so that Satan does not tempt you because of your lack of self-control." God stresses the importance of mutuality in a healthy sexual relationship between the husband and the wife. When marriage is what it should be, with the husband and wife loving and respecting each other, and neither of them ever having been abused, this passage is much easier to understand and follow.

---

80   This phenomenon is explored in more depth in the article "When the wife was sexually abused as a child: Marital relations before and during her therapy for abuse," by Sheri Oz, *Sexual and Relationship Therapy*, August 25, 2010, pp. 287-298.

However, for abuse survivors, the thought of someone else having authority over their body can be terrifying, because the offender forced himself on them and on their bodies, stealing something very precious that God never intended him to have. That was evil and wrong and is something that God hates.

In some cases the spouse is aware of the abuse and at least knows the reason for some of their struggles. In many cases, though, the one who was abused never shares with the spouse what has happened, so the spouse has no idea why they are struggling, not only in their sex life, but with intimacy in general. This causes doubt, frustration, anger, mistrust, resentment, and pain in the marriage. In her book *Not Marked,* Mary DeMuth describes the pain of trying to keep up a charade of enjoying sex during her early married years, only to find that façade eventually come crashing down.[81]

Often for the victims, sex and sexual activity are something they have come to despise and dread. Many of the chronic problems in marriage, such as sexual brokenness, pornography, unfaithfulness, lack of trust, poor communication, anger, and fighting are often the aftermath of sexual abuse. Many unhealthy marriages result from an offender's sin. This may be one of the reasons that the concept of mutual submission is so difficult for many to accept.[82] Both the spouse and the one who was abused need to prayerfully seek a greater

---

81   Mary DeMuth, *Not Marked: Finding Hope and Healing after Sexual Abuse* (Uncaged Publishing, 2013), Kindle edition.

82   The word *submit* does mean "to be under obedience." In a godly marriage, mutual submission works because the husband and wife love and respect each other. Submission works the way God intends when the strongest force in a marriage is real love.

understanding of God and his Word, as well as the devastation of sexual abuse and how it will impact their marriage.

But what about when the abuse is perpetrated by the husband? We have heard of many cases in which the wife has been told to stay in a relationship even if it is abusive. But there's no place in God's Word where He tells the wife to submit to abuse, or to subject her children to abuse. We have even heard from women who were told by their pastor or church leaders to stay in these harmful situations; some church leaders have said that a wife should not leave an abusive husband even if he actually does kill her.[83] But abuse toward the wife breaks the marriage covenant. Our churches should not turn a blind eye to sexual abuse and violence within a marriage. On the contrary, our churches should lead the way in supporting the victim in order to deliver the oppressed out of the hand of the oppressor. Leslie Vernick, whose admonitions to women in destructive relationships apply specifically to those being sexually abused, has said,

> Counselors and pastors often advise a wife that God calls her to suffer in her marriage while continuing to provide all the privileges and benefits of marriage regardless of how her husband treats her, provides for her, or violates their marital vows. This stance only reinforces the delusion that the destructive spouse who believes he can do as he pleases with no consequences. Marriage does not give someone a "get-out-of-jail free" card that entitles a husband to lie,

---

83   This was said by church elders to a friend, a woman in an abusive marriage.

mistreat, ignore, be cruel, or crush his wife's God-given dignity without any consequences.[84]

Sexual abuse can have powerful and long-lasting effects on a marriage. But it also causes consequences to the abuse survivor's children.

It was November of 2005, and Faith's father had been caught molesting his foster granddaughter. Faith wasn't going to let him get away with it this time.

She wrote letters about her abuse to send to her eight brothers and her mother. She had to let them know.

As soon as they knew, all our five children would find out. So she had to tell them too.

One by one she told them. It was hard, but for the sake of her foster niece, she had to do it.

Then next day our children were talking among themselves, trying to process the abuse and the effect it had had on their childhood.

One of them said, "That explains a lot."

When Faith tells her story in churches and colleges, she shares that the years of rape and abuse by her father caused her to die emotionally. Even though Faith was always a kind and loving wife and mother, she was emotionally wounded. Our children missed out on a lot because their mother didn't express joy or excitement very well— she seldom cried or spoke out in public. The ripple effect of this one man's sin seems to have kept on going throughout the family.

---

84   Leslie Vernick, *The Emotionally Destructive Marriage: How to Find Your Voice and Reclaim Your Hope* (Waterbrook Press, 2013), p. 157.

"One of the best tests for joyful group identity is a high concentration of hopeful daughters. Joyful little girls who love the way that babies, women, mothers, and wives are treated by both men and women in their culture will look forward to starting joyful families of their own. Hopeful daughters will grow a joyful generation and joyful group identity. . . . Girls' joy levels let us accurately predict the future for families, churches, and schools of the region."[85]

What a tragedy when our little girls grow up with just the opposite.

REPERCUSSIONS FOR THE OFFENDER

The abuse survivor who wrote about how she felt in the previous section ended her letter this way:

> *I don't understand why we have to carry the stench and filth, and the offenders smell nice and beautiful??? They manage to look so good and never seem to have to be uncovered/humiliated.*[86]

Chapter 5, "Understand the Enablers," explores some of the reasons that a shockingly small percentage of sexual offenders are convicted (some estimates range as low as three percent).[87] In addition, recent court trials that have made the national news tell stories of judges who have sentenced convicted sex offenders to outrageously light sentences or no prison time at all.[88] The first thing to cross my

---

85   E. James Wilder, et al, *Joy Starts Here*, p. 79.

86   Personal correspondence, used by permission.

87   From the website of the Rape, Abuse, and Incest National Network (RAINN), www.rainn.org/statistics.

88   See, for example, Ashley Alman, "One Percenter Convicted Of Raping Child Dodges Jail Because He 'Will Not Fare Well,'" The Huffington Post, April 1, 2014, accessed via http://www.huffingtonpost.com/2014/03/30/robert-richards-rape_n_5060386.html.

mind is to wonder if the judge himself is an abuser. When a child has been so horribly abused and the offender is found guilty yet the judge only slaps him on the wrist, we can't help but wonder why. It could be that in this life we won't see the justice system carry through to bring justice to a sexual offender as it should. But God is the ultimate judge.

In 2 Samuel 12:10, Nathan the prophet told David that because of his sins of adultery and murder, "the sword shall never depart from your house." God even went on to say that he would raise up an adversary against David from his own house. When David confessed his sin and asked for God's forgiveness and fully repented, God did forgive him, but the consequences were still meted out by God and by those around David whom God used to hold him accountable for what he had done. David's life is a sobering reminder that sin brings consequences.

When Jesus said in Luke 17:2 that it would be better for a person to have a millstone hung around his neck and be thrown into the sea than that he should offend one of these little ones, clearly he was talking about abuse. Whether physical, emotional, spiritual, or sexual abuse, Jesus was outraged at the thought of someone offending a child, and pronounced "woe" upon anyone who would do such a thing. When he deals with those who rape and molest children, it will no doubt be a terrifying event.

Romans 1 gives us the grave reminder that sin upon sin leads to more and more of a hardening of conscience and deeper sin. This in itself should be enough of a warning to those of us who love God to pull the offender out of the path of destruction that he is on.[89]

---

89   Practical action is described in Chapters 10 and 11, "What Our Churches Must Do" and "What the Offender Must Do."

REPERCUSSIONS FOR OUR
CHURCHES AND FOR SOCIETY

If over twenty percent of the people of our society have experienced sexual assault or molestation,[90] then by examining the effects on the victim and on the families, considering the fact that the majority of offenders are never incarcerated, we can see what an extremely deleterious effect this crime will have on our society, contributing to its destruction at its very root. But this fact becomes even more sobering when we consider that the crime is in our churches, hiding in plain sight.

One church in Michigan, where the pastor was arrested for abusing a child, told us that afterwards a number of parents in the community told their children, "That's why we don't go to church." I wonder how many people stay away from church because of the ungodliness they see from the people who attend. For many outside our churches, rather than seeing a beacon of light drawing them to Christ, they see only the hypocrisy eclipsing the light. This refusal to acknowledge sin all too often turns people away, especially the ones most needing healing.

Our churches are quick to condemn the evils of society. Pastors speak passionately against the wrong of abortion, for example, as well they should. But these same leaders can be willfully blind to the needs of the souls among us who are often haunted by a deep self-hatred and what many of them consider to be a shameful secret.

---

90   Statistics show that about 20% of the population report having been raped or molested before reaching their eighteenth birthday. More are raped or molested after their eighteenth birthday, raising the number significantly. And of course, there may be many who have never admitted that they have been violated.

First Samuel 4 tells the sad story of an old priest named Eli who had two very wicked sons who took sexual advantage of the women who came to the tabernacle. Because of their great evil, which included profaning the holy Ark of the Covenant, God allowed Israel to be defeated, the two sons to be killed, and the Ark of God to be taken by the enemies. When Eli's daughter-in-law gave birth, she named the child "Ichabod," which means "the glory of the Lord is departed."

I doubt that there has ever been a pastor who didn't pray for God's blessing on his church and ministry. But how can God possibly bless a church that stubbornly refuses to deal with this gross moral depravity? In many churches today where the wickedness of some is being protected by the silence of others, maybe "Ichabod" should be written over the doors.

Will we face the repercussions of this serious crime? Are we willing to call offenders to account? Are we willing to be the hands and feet of Jesus to offer hope and lovingly bind the wounds of those who may be afraid they're beyond hope? Will we walk with them on a healing journey that may be circuitous and difficult, as one of the deepest displays of love?

What will be the repercussions for our churches if we don't?

CHAPTER 5

UNDERSTAND THE ENABLERS

Although the sins of sexual abuse are committed by criminal offenders, a natural question arises: why are they seldom caught, and how can they manage to go from one victim to another without the unsuspecting public finding out? There are several reasons, but one of the most common is the presence and subtle assistance of enablers, who themselves are sinning by covering the crime, and in some cases are also committing a criminal offense.[91]

Most people who protect the perpetrators and blame and shame the victims probably never think of themselves as enablers in the matter of heinous crimes. But when a sexual offender finds his next victim because of the aid of those who ignored God's warning, these enablers are in effect sometimes even as culpable as the offender.

---

91   Though in cases of mandatory reporting it is a criminal offense to cover the sexual assault of a minor, many enablers are committing sexual sins, and even crimes, of their own. For example, the leaders of the First Baptist Church of Hammond, Indiana, covered the crimes of offenders in their church for years, several of whom were eventually exposed. In 2012, the pastor of the church, Jack Schaap, one of the primary enablers, was himself arrested for statutory rape. An excellent *Chicago Magazine* article on the subject can be accessed at www.chicagomag. com, "Let Us Prey: Big Trouble at First Baptist Church," January 2013.

Both direct enablers—those who take action to protect the perpetrator—as well as indirect enablers—those who remain silent to protect the perpetrator—are guilty before God.

When the right way to go lies in front of a person, but he or she purposely chooses to go a different way, this is sin. "Therefore," says James 4:17, "to him who knows to do good and does not do it, to him it is sin."

DIRECT ENABLERS

Direct enablers are those who get involved in the situation. They take action. They make phone calls; they write letters. They give convincing arguments to try to get others involved on behalf of the offender. They might even hire lawyers. They do all this in an effort to minimize the consequences for the offender.

But why do they do it?

Motivated by a desire to protect the offender

"He's such a nice man"

"Brenda, Faith's dad is going to have to stop leading the group at your house." I was speaking into the phone. With our very naïve lack of understanding of repentance and forgiveness, Faith's father had been allowed to lead a small group for years, but now things were different. "He's just confessed to molesting a teenage girl."

There was a long pause. When Brenda spoke, I could tell she was crying. "We can't let the church know."

"They have to know. He's going to be arrested; it's going to be in the papers."

"But they can't know yet. Not yet."

In spite of Brenda's unreasonable protest, I proceeded with a public announcement. A month later when Faith and I were out of town, she raised her hand in church at testimony time. "I just want to praise the Lord that we have four wonderful pastors here." Who was she talking about? We were a small church, and I was the only pastor.

Hmmm. Besides me, there was the retired pastor, my brother-in-law who preached sometimes, and . . . Faith's dad.

Recently we've been working with a group of believers in a church where the pastor molested a fourteen-year-old girl in the youth group. He pled guilty to the charges and received three weeks in jail. When the church met to address the issue, some of the people thought they should give the pastor a second chance. What does that mean? A second chance to do what? A second chance to get it right? A second chance to minister? Or would it really be a second chance to rape and molest another child?

In one recent case involving a pastor who had molested two children, the pastor's wife blamed the church people, saying that they weren't praying hard enough for their pastor. It was easier for her to blame the church than to hold her husband accountable. As outrageous as this behavior is, it is not uncommon. Blind loyalty to a pastor or ministry leader is encouraged and even demanded in many so-called Christian organizations. To question the leader is tantamount to questioning Christ. To actively work to protect the leader is working to "protect the cause of Christ."

Jeri Massi, a researcher who has documented over a hundred cases of abuse in fundamentalist churches, wrote,

> I believe that there are Fundamentalist churches that hand so much power to a man and feed his massive, disordered ego and appetites [so much] that he is free to fall deeper into the grossest of sins. And the "good" churches do not stop them, identify them, or expel them. They do not even warn other churches of the nomadic molesters who get expelled from one pulpit and go out seeking the next. That behavior does enable and even empowers evil men.[92]

The power dynamic in these situations cannot be overlooked. Not only has the offender held a position of perceived power over the abuse victim, but all too often he also holds a position of perceived authority over the people who become his enablers. If he is a large donor to the church, the pastor may often hasten to become the first enabler. If he is the pastor himself, especially in an environment that is already spiritually abusive, the power dynamic keeps the congregation from questioning him.

> There are spiritual systems in which what people think, how they feel, and what they need or want does not matter. . ... In these systems, the members are there to meet the needs of the leaders: needs for power, importance, intimacy, value—really, self-related needs. These leaders attempt to find fulfillment through the religious performance of the

---

92   Jeri Massi, *Schizophrenic Christianity: How Christian Fundamentalism Attracts and Protects Sociopaths, Abusive Pastors, and Child Molesters* (Jupiter Rising Books, 2014), Kindle edition.

very people whom they are there to serve and build. This is an inversion in the body of Christ. It is spiritual abuse.[93]

When an offender or church is confronted with the evidence of this sin, and when the sin can no longer be denied or excused, the enablers may attempt to minimize the sin and convince others that it's not really as bad as it appears. They may refer to statutory rape or child abuse as a "mutual relationship" or "an affair." But sexually abusing anyone is evil and wrong and should be recognized and called by the filthy name it deserves.

There was Brenda the Enabler, coming toward us in Wal-Mart. She was going to give us a hug. She always did that, every time she saw us. Usually we gritted our teeth and endured it.

But this time was different. This time I had had enough. I held up my hand like a police officer. "Don't hug us and pretend you love us when you're condoning his behavior."

She stopped short and fumbled, embarrassed. "Oh, I don't condone his behavior."

"By your actions you're condoning his abuse," I said. "You even know what he did to Faith, but you're trying to get the home group to welcome him back. You're talking about what a wonderful pastor he is when he hasn't even repented. By your very actions you're condoning what he does, and your actions are speaking a lot louder than your words."

---

93   David Johnson and Jeff VanVonderen, *The Subtle Power of Spiritual Abuse: Recognizing and Escaping Spiritual Manipulation and False Spiritual Authority Within the Church* (Minneapolis: Bethany House, 2005), p. 23.

We should have confronted Brenda with her sin officially as a
church body. But she left the church.

For the sake of the offenders themselves, as well as the victims
and the churches and society, it's time for protection of offenders to
come to an end.

Motivated by self-preservation

"We don't want to hurt the ministry"

When a case of sexual abuse becomes known, it seems that the
first thought of some ministry leaders is "How will this affect me or
my organization?"

In a similar scenario of a potentially catastrophic crisis, in 1982
Tylenol capsules on store shelves were found to be purposely laced
with cyanide (a sociopathic crime), causing several innocent people
to die terrible deaths. In a refreshingly different response than we
often see from corporations,

> Johnson & Johnson chairman, James Burke, reacted to the
> negative media coverage by forming a seven-member strat-
> egy team. The team's strategy guidance from Burke was
> first, "How do we protect the people?" and second "How do
> we save this product?"[94]

Though the way through was difficult, Johnson & Johnson, by its
integrity in dealing with the situation, restored Tylenol's good name.
Sadly this response is seldom the case in Christian circles. Leaders

---

94   Department of Defense, "Case Study: The Johnson & Johnson Tylenol Crisis," Crisis Communication Strategies, http://www.ou.edu/deptcomm/dodjcc/
groups/o2C2/Johnson%20&%20Johnson.htmCase Study: The Johnson & Johnson Tylenol Crisis.

often think the best response is to get this situation over as quickly and quietly as possible. Damage-control mode kicks in to "protect the ministry," keeping the scandal of abuse in house. In many church communities, instead of dealing with the sin and the offender who has caused so much hurt, the choice is to look the other way, "for the collective good."

Many Christians depend on their church leaders to deal with the sexual offender, but often, for reasons of self-protection, the leaders never call the authorities to report this as a crime. At one of our conferences, a lady told us that years before, her children had been molested by the youth pastor. When she and her husband went to the leaders of the church about it, she told us, "they practiced shunning . . . they shunned us!" Nothing was done to the youth pastor. No action was taken against the perpetrator of the crime.

One abuse survivor told us about rampant sexual abuse by a faculty member of a Christian school that was reported to the church leaders. But the pastor warned these congregants to be quiet or there would be consequences. To this woman's knowledge, these cases of sexual assault were never reported to the authorities, and as far as we know at the time of this writing, that faculty member is still employed by that school. The consequences of such perpetrator protection are devastating.

It could be that the pastor wants to protect a ministry that he thinks is valuable. But when he decides to cover a crime and enable the offender, he becomes an accessory to that crime and presents a completely false picture of God's character. Any value his ministry may have has been lost, and the ministry will become a hollow shell.

Church leaders often fear that a scandal will hurt **attendance**. Since many churches are constantly competing and searching for people to attend their churches, leaders often feel that anything that might be a threat to church growth must be avoided, believing that their church must have the best "image." They think they can't take the chance that they might lose members.

A member of our church molested his granddaughter.

I was the pastor.

The molester was my father-in-law.

We confronted him, two and then more together. No real repentance. No fruits of repentance.

Then we had to bring it out into the open. Announce it to the church. Practice church discipline.

And people left. Many people left.

To be frank, at the time of this writing, our church has not recovered the number of members we had before 2006.

Did we do the wrong thing? No, we did the right thing, because the right thing was to be like Jesus in standing with the ones who had been offended. The right thing was to go after the one lost sheep, as Jesus did. And through that experience, Speaking Truth in Love Ministries was born.

Our church has thrived, not in numbers, but in compassion.

Sometimes a desire to protect **reputation** motivates a self-preserving enabler. When the victim and the offender are in the same family, the victim often has no advocate, because the ones who should be protecting the victim decide that the reputation of the family is more important than the victim's safety or justice.

"Mom," I said to Faith's mother, "I have to tell you something."

She could tell by the sound of my voice that it wasn't going to be anything good.

"You know that Dad molested Alyssa."

She stared straight ahead, not speaking.

"Well, Dad molested Faith when she was a child. He raped her."

We loved Mom and respected her. Through all the years, she had worked hard to support her family, and she seemed to want to do the right thing. So her reaction surprised me—she began to cry angrily.

"We'll lose our good reputation! We'll lose our home! We'll lose everything I've worked for all these years!"

"Mom, didn't you hear what I—"

She cut me off, crying. "You don't understand! This is about our family's good name!"

"No, Mom," I said. "You're the one who doesn't understand. Somehow you're not getting what it was that your husband did to your daughter."

It wasn't long after that—the same night I told the hospital where he was Volunteer Clergy why he was no longer "clergy" with our church—that we got the midnight call.

Faith picked up the phone.

"When is this going to stop?!" the voice at the other end screamed. "When will you stop these attacks?"

"Mom, it wasn't—"

"When will you stop? It's just going on and on and on! We'll lose everything!"

"But Mom, Dad is the one—"

"We're not going to talk about it," the voice said abruptly. The line went dead.

Heitritter and Vought describe another mother's reaction: "Mrs. Taylor looked intently at her thirteen-year-old daughter and asked, 'How could you do this to me? You took my husband away, and you have ruined the family.'"[95] Responses like these to an initial effort to speak will often serve to silence a victim for decades.

In the case of the abuse at the Mamou Alliance Academy in West Africa, some of the leaders actively covered up the abuse so that the organization's image wouldn't be tarnished.[96] Boz Tchividjian, whose organization GRACE (Godly Response to Abuse in the Christian

---

95   Heitritter and Vought, *Helping Victims of Sexual Abuse*, p. 78.

96   *All God's Children*, DVD, 2008, www.allgodschildrenthefilm.com.

Environment)[97] conducted investigations into sexual abuse on mission fields, said,

> Institutional-centered cultures will often place institutional reputation over individual value. To this end, such institutions commonly erect . . . walls of silence upon learning of allegations related to child abuse. The first wall silences members from even mentioning allegations of abuse. This institutional directive is often under the guise of preventing "gossip," when oftentimes the real reason is the institution's desire to protect its status and reputation among its members. A culture that silences members from speaking with each other about suspected abuse is one where abuse will almost always flourish.[98]

The leaders of both large and small ministries also fear **lawsuits** when someone has been abused by a church leader or a staff member. There may be times when the abuse survivor or family will sue the church no matter how carefully the church tries to handle things right from the beginning, but we know of no instances like that. Christians who have been sexually assaulted by ministry leaders want for the church to follow through with justice as much as possible by turning the offender over to the law and holding him accountable before the church, to express heartfelt sorrow for the trauma caused to the victim and any part they played in it, and to express love and

---

97   www.netgrace.org.

98   Basyle "Boz" Tchividjian, "Walls of Silence: Protecting the institution over the individual," http://netgrace.org/walls-of-silence-protecting-the-institution-over-the-individual, May 1, 2012.

encouragement for the abuse survivors, expressing that they wanted to help the abuse survivor however they could.

We know of a number of adults who have said that even though the ministry handled their abuse situation very badly in the past, the main thing they wanted now was a heartfelt apology and genuine sorrow.[99] But when churches and ministries respond inappropriately or not at all, abuse survivors often feel that they have no recourse but to sue in order to receive justice and bring people's attention to the problem.

Of course, loss of attendance, loss of reputation, and impending lawsuits will all very likely affect the **finances** of an organization. A church or other ministry may never financially recover from a sexual abuse scandal. Ministry leaders must honestly, before God, ask themselves serious questions:

Is my job more important than vulnerable souls?

Is God working only through this facility?

Does the fear of this organization losing income mean that I won't support abuse victims?

Am I going to build a wall of protection around this sin in order to continue the cash flow?

How much money is it worth for me to refuse to face the sin in our midst?

---

99   Christa Brown expresses this sentiment in *This Little Light*, p. 117. The Vienna Presbyterian Church got it right. After mishandling cases of clear abuse, they defied their lawyers and publicly sought forgiveness and restitution to the abuse victims. As of this writing, no charges against them have been filed. See Josh White, "Vienna Presbyterian Church seeks forgiveness, redemption in wake of abuse scandal," *The Washington Post*, April 2, 2011.

What kind of dollar value are we putting on the souls of the vulnerable among us?

Dealing justly with an abuse report can be costly. It is a situation that calls for us to be strong and courageous in Christ, realizing that he promises to be with us in it all. Many people who profess to be Christians simply are not willing to pay the price.[100]

Yet is this not the work of Jesus? Are there churches and ministries that are willing to pay that price? Are there some who will forego having a ministry that looks neat and clean from the outside in order to actively be the hands and feet of Jesus?

One much darker story at work here is that many of our Christian leaders are hiding gross sins in their own lives, and they fear **exposure**. Their sin may not be sexual abuse, but they may be hiding pornography, adultery, embezzlement, or a host of other sins, even crimes.[101] If they were to move forward with exposing the sin of sexual abuse, they fear that their own misdeeds may also be exposed. For their own self-preservation, to protect from self-incrimination, these ministry leaders seek to cover the sin. From the lack in interest in dealing with the issue that we've seen in many Christian organizations, this appears to be a major problem.

---

100   Crippen and Wood, *A Cry for Justice*, p. 175.

101   For example, Bill Gothard, a highly respected leader in evangelical circles, stepped down from his organization, Institute in Basic Life Principles, in 2014. His brother had been involved in gross immorality, and Gothard, who covered for him, was later exposed as having been involved in sexual harassment and other sexually inappropriate treatment of subordinates, as well as other abuses of authority. See "The GOTHARD Files: The Scandal, 1980" at www.recov?inggrace.org.

Closely related to the fear of exposure is the sin of **cronyism**. The only way that sexual abuse within an organization can go on for so long in a larger convention, organization, or network of churches without being exposed is if there is a cooperative effort by those in the inner circles to cover it up. This is more than just one buddy watching out for another; it is deeming "loyalty" rather than love to be the greatest strength a Christian can display.

Offenders who are deemed to be valuable or "loyal" to the organization or church or ministry will often simply be moved elsewhere in hopes that the situation will be forgotten. And again we see that the high-profile wrongdoers are valued more than the ones they have wounded. For example, a Christian college may count on a certain large church to send them students. Then, when the son of the pastor, a student at the college, seduces and rapes an underage girl, the pastor and leaders of the college work together to cover the crime. Because of the mutual loyalty, both the pastor and the president of the college will publicly praise each other, while in the darkness working together to hide the sins that may cause them to suffer loss of attendance, loss of reputation, and loss of finances. They seek to clean up the mess and shake hands on it. And they may even praise the young offender from the pulpit—who has gone on to another ministry.

Motivated by a misguided desire to help

"You just need to forgive"

Many Christians actively cover the sin of sexual abuse because they fear it will cause pain and suffering for the victim and the victim's family. Throughout the abuse the criminal offender has been telling the victim, usually with threats, "Don't tell anyone." Now, the well-meaning "helper" enabler echoes those words to the victim: "He has repented. You have forgiven. Now don't ever say anything about it again." This echo of the abuser's words will serve to further confuse and demoralize and degrade the abuse survivor, as he or she continues to struggle with the fallout from the abuse while watching the perpetrator be restored with a quick pseudo-repentance, often even to his former position.

Sometimes there is a well-intentioned desire to shield the one who was victimized. If the assault hasn't yet been reported to the police, some misguided helper-enablers may urge the abuse survivor or the family not to do so, because they believe that would cause more pain and trauma for the survivor and embarrassment for the family and would in some cases break up a family and remove the primary breadwinner. They may also try to keep the survivor from testifying in court because of how difficult it would be to go through the trial. It's true—the trial can be very difficult, even traumatic. But when the course of justice is curtailed, then the healing process can be affected as well.[102]

All of these potentialities are truly painful. Following the course of justice may be very difficult for the survivor. It may embarrass

---

102   Though we believe justice is an important goal, we also believe that adult survivors should know that they are free to make the decision themselves of whether or not to report the crime, depending on a number of factors, without feeling a burden of guilt. Counseling through a local rape crisis center (or other counseling center recommended by rape crisis counselors) is a valuable resource for abuse survivors as this decision is being considered. If they choose to report, they should be assured that they will be supported and encouraged during every step of the journey. While pressure should not be placed on the abuse survivor, it is completely appropriate to "pressure" the offender to turn himself in to the authorities and fully confess his crime. His confession and guilty plea will spare his victims from the agony of having to report the crime themselves. This process is further discussed in Chapter 11, "What the Offender Must Do."

the family. It may break up the family. It may remove the primary breadwinner. The plain fact is, though, that toxic waste never goes away. The deeper and wider toxic waste is buried, the more pain and trouble it causes as it leaks out in unexpected ways, and the more damage is ultimately done. Once the toxicity of abuse has occurred, there is no painless solution. It must be fully dealt with in order for the abuse survivor to find lasting healing.

Well-meaning people may often tell abuse survivors to "just leave the past in the past." But this shows a stark misunderstanding not only of the continued effect that trauma has on the life of the survivor (in a flashback, for example, the past becomes the present), but also of the ongoing abuse. One abuse survivor said, "It's not in the past. . .. How can it be in the past when he's still in the pulpit and could still hurt others?"[103] Another abuse survivor wrote:

> For a long time I stifled my questions, believing they were wrong. I was pretty sure that if I ever opened the door to those questions, my church would condemn me. The times that a few of them leaked out, I was met with the verses about forgiveness, forgetting the past, life being about eternity rather than present hardships, etc. They answered my questions for a bit. I would re-determine to keep the past in the past and stay focused on eternity, etc. It didn't stop the nightmares. Eventually it all burst out in a flood of confusion, fear, guilt, shame, etc. None of the questions had truly been answered. They were just hidden deep in a sea of confusion. I didn't think that church was where I could find answers. I was sure that I would find only condemnation for the

---

questions. I tried to keep them silent, but I was dying inside. All of these things were blocking a real, genuine, trusting relationship with God, and no amount of just confessing them as sin fixed it.[104]

One of the most damaging effects of the helper-enabler can come in the form of **destructive counseling**.

Well-meaning teachers in Christian youth groups and colleges and camps—who readily talk about sex outside of marriage but don't seem to want to talk about sexual abuse—have said that having sex before marriage can compare to being like a chewed-up piece of gum, or water that has been spit in. When a speaker draws no distinction between the one who voluntarily participates in sex and the one who is tricked or forced into sex, the shame on the sexual abuse victim can be devastating.[105]

I was molested by a police officer as a child, so I was horrified that [a professor at the Christian university I attended] taught in my freshman psychology class that women or girls who were molested should confess the sin of the past that they "enjoyed." I told no one about the molestation until I was almost forty years old.[106]

If the wicked offender's sexual abuse isn't addressed directly and clearly as a heinous crime in God's eyes in these venues—and why shouldn't it be?—then other teachings can communicate to victims

---

104   Personal correspondence, used by permission.

105   See Alex Dominguez, "Elizabeth Smart speaks on human trafficking," *The Christian Science Monitor,* May 4, 2013, accessed at http://www.csmonitor.com/USA/Latest-News-Wires/2013/0504/Elizabeth-Smart-speaks-on-human-trafficking. Though Elizabeth Smart was raised in Mormon culture, the teaching about sexual purity in many fundamentalist and evangelical circles is very similar to the teaching in which she was raised.

106   Personal correspondence, used by permission.

that they should simply endure the abusive situation. The teaching that the abused body is the "throwaway part" of the self, unimportant as compared to the soul and the spirit, can exponentially increase the shame and confusion in a person who has been abused.[107] "Christians don't have any rights" is another key teaching that has silenced victims who fear God.[108]

When survivors finally disclose abuse from their past, they are often already very confused and in emotional turmoil, filled with questions and doubts, needing a safe place to work through their struggles. Their story is a tender piece of the soul and is not given without a price. They need to be assured that their words are sacred words that will be held with care. Even lay counselors, small group leaders, or friends need to understand what an honor it is to hear an abuse survivor's story, which may have been under lock and key for decades.

When survivors finally disclose, tremendous power is carried in the first words they hear and the first reaction they encounter. That power, which can be used to encourage and uplift, with the ability to

---

107   See, for example, Bob Wood, *Scriptural Principles for Counseling the Abused*, DVD (Greenville, SC: Bob Jones University, 1994). This counseling class, though over twenty years old, was still advertised for sale in the Bob Jones University catalogs as recently as 2013.

108   In Nancy Leigh DeMoss's book *Lies Women Believe and the Truth that Sets Them Free* (Chicago: Moody Press, 2001), she says on page 74, "The fact is, successful relationships and healthy cultures are not built on the *claiming* of rights but on the *yielding* of rights." These words, spoken by this popular writer and radio host in a book used to counsel women, are devastating to those whose most basic personal rights have been violated by sexual abuse. She continues on the next page to mock anyone who believes in rights, saying sarcastically, "if any of your rights are violated, you have a right to protest. You have a right to be angry. . ... You have right to take action. You have a right to insist on your rights!" Her clearly-stated message to abuse survivors is that they have no rights. This is essentially what their offender has told them all along. These are absolutely crushing words.

help set them on a journey toward healing and hope, is all too often used to heap on more guilt and shame, potentially pushing them into a pit of hopelessness.

Many Christian organizations will discourage victims of abuse from going to counselors who are licensed specifically in treatment of trauma, claiming that counsel that is not exclusively from the Bible will turn the abuse survivor away from God. But trauma counseling is often exactly what abuse survivors need, and will not preclude others lovingly pointing them to the ultimate hope that they can find in Jesus Christ.

The first way a Christian counselor can devastate abuse survivors who comes for help is by showing disbelief, even sometimes accusing them of lying. ("It couldn't possibly have been as bad as you say.") We know of more than one case in which this has happened. It has served to shut up survivors for years, preventing healing.[109]

A lack of understanding of the deep devastation that sexual abuse causes in the life of the victim often results in ministry leaders failing to take sufficient time to listen as the victim seeks to process the trauma and sort through the confusion. Many times these counselors don't understand the deeply imbedded lies that need to be patiently and lovingly replaced with truth, again and again and again.

Instead, destructive counseling will quickly try to fix the problem by focusing on perceived sin that the victim needs to repent of: perceived sin committed in the aftermath of the abuse, and even,

---

109 A counselor's primary responsibility might be seen as helping the client to replace lies with truth. This would not include the counselor making a determination about the facts of the abuse, which the counselor didn't observe, and which is the responsibility of others.

incredibly, "sin" committed during the abuse itself. During this extremely critical juncture in a very vulnerable person's life, some counselors in their ignorance use the Bible to heap more shame and blame on one who has been traumatized, causing far more confusion and harm.[110]

It's not uncommon for Christian counselors to blame the abuse victim for the perceived sin of "your part" in the sexual abuse—including questioning what the victim was wearing, questioning whether the victim "cried out" loudly when the assailant overpowered him or her, and questioning any physical/biological response to the act of rape, which they say should be repented of. This shaming can silence a victim for years, preventing healing.

Christian counselors can also blame abuse victims for what they perceive to be sin in the aftermath of the abuse,[111] as evidence that the abuse survivor has not forgiven. Anorexia and cutting are often treated as sins as well. Abuse survivors are told by some counselors

---

110   The worksheet "Counseling Sexual Abuse" published by the Advanced Training Institute blames the victim for, among other things, failing to report. The worksheet quotes Deuteronomy 22:22-26., showing an appalling lack of understanding of the trauma a sexually violated person often experiences after a sexual assault, trauma which may immobilize him or her from being able to report. The abuse victim should never have to take the responsibility of the weight of guilt for the possibility that others may be abused. In this worksheet the sexual assault survivor is also admonished to clear his or her "guilt" before God, with a reference to 1 John 1:9. (This worksheet is another example of counseling that de-personalizes the offender, referring to the abuse only in the passive voice, e.g., "Failing to report it allows others to be abused.") Full worksheet can be accessed at the Recovering Grace website, "How 'Counseling Sexual Abuse' Blames and Shames Survivors," www.recoveringgrace.org, April 18, 2013.

111   The perceived sin in the aftermath is often the normal response to trauma discussed in Chapter 4, or very natural struggles with anger and the goodness and presence of God at the time of the crime. Rather than opportunities for condemnation, these struggles should be seen as opportunities for counselors and others to show compassion for the abuse survivors and point them to the loving Shepherd, Jesus Christ. See more about this in Chapter 12, "How Family and Friends Must Help."

that continued problems such as these are indications that they haven't truly forgiven or that they are allowing a "root of bitterness" to grow in their lives.[112] Then they will be assigned Bible verses about forgiveness to read and/or memorize.[113] Though forgiveness is important,[114] what is often meant by this immediate emphasis on forgiveness is "stuff your pain and keep your mouth shut." Forcing victims to simply utter words of forgiveness and keep silent can be likened to shutting them away in an isolated prison cell. This isolation can silence a victim for years, preventing healing.

One counselor, preaching to hundreds of young people, told about a teenage girl who had been molested by her stepfather for two years. In describing his counseling with her, he told his response: "Young lady, you've lived a very difficult life. A very hard life." Then, instead of describing appropriate compassion for this young woman who had not been protected by those who should have protected her, he said, "But let's look at your sin in this situation." He then described how he told her that she needed to repent of her anger, hatred, and bitterness. Instead of demonstrating a heart of compassion and showing her a picture of Jesus' love for her in her condition of brokenness, he immediately diagnosed the problem to be . . . her. He even turned

---

112   The accusation of bitterness is based on Hebrews 12:15, "looking carefully lest anyone fall short of the grace of God; lest any root of bitterness springing up cause trouble, and by this many become defiled." This verse has been grossly misapplied to people who have been horribly victimized, in an effort to urge them to forgive before they have even had the opportunity to process their trauma, to even understand what it is they are forgiving.

113   We love the Bible and believe it is an important source of healing and hope for abuse survivors, but we believe that it's wrong to use the Bible to shame and blame abuse victims and heap on more guilt.

114   The concept of forgiveness is dealt with more fully in chapter 8, "Believe and Speak the Truth about Forgiveness."

the tables on her and admonished her to seek forgiveness of her abusive stepfather for her anger toward him.[115]

Far too many Christians think that once abuse survivors have had a few meetings and memorized some Bible verses and "repented of their part" in the abuse and spoken words of forgiveness to or about the offender, that everything should be solved. Abuse survivors—and everyone else—should be able to get on with their lives. But do we tell someone who has been physically maimed for life because of a sadistic act of violence that they're bitter and unforgiving, or that they're not trying hard enough, because their body isn't healed right away? Yet it would appear that this is exactly what many church leaders and experts are telling those who have been emotionally, physically, and psychologically devastated by sexual abuse.

That fact is that damaging counsel is often a mask for the extreme level of discomfort that leaders can feel when faced with such horrific accusations. The easiest thing to do is to shame and blame the already-vulnerable victims, pressuring them to keep quiet. This causes unimaginable additional damage and pain to the ones who have already been wounded. It seems to be a rare thing for a church or other ministry to actually love and support abuse survivors by listening without condemnation, showing unwavering compassion, and being patient when the healing process takes time. But weeping with those who weep and walking the sometimes painfully slow journey of healing with abuse survivors is what the Church of Jesus Christ is called to do. It is vital for abuse survivors to have the opportunity

---

115   Rand Hummel, "Religious Robots: A Mechanical Walk with God," September 4, 2009, accessed at www.sermonaudio.com.

to share openly what they've been through with someone they can trust, because after such horrific trauma they need validation that they really do matter, and they need to know that someone cares enough to listen.

Destructive counseling adds exponentially to the confusion, fear, and shame for abuse survivors. Many have said that this shame-based counseling has been at least as traumatizing to them as the original offense. This offers a significant reason why many survivors, after initially reporting the crime and facing such destructive counseling, are afraid to come forward again, even decades after it happened.[116]

And the abuse continues.

In the end, the "helper-enablers" help no one. They only allow the toxicity of abuse to continue to poison the landscape of Christianity.

INDIRECT ENABLERS

Indirect enablers are those who hear about abuse but do nothing at all. They don't want to talk about it; they want to pretend that it didn't happen or that it will just go away. They may think, after all, those things happened in the past and "there is nothing that can be done about it now." Though this kind of wall of silence can seem more benign, just like the direct enablers these people can also ultimately devastate the abuse survivor, the family, the church, and our society.

---

116   We pray that Christians will be quick to recommend that abuse survivors who are struggling with the re-victimization of destructive counseling seek professionally licensed counselors who have dedicated their studies and practice to victims of trauma, specifically sexual abuse if possible, or if that is not possible, others that trauma counselors recommend.

Isaiah 59:1–4 recounts Israel's sinful state and sinful way of life, including the fact that "No one calls for justice, nor does any plead for truth." They simply ignored the pleas of innocent victims. To our shame, the same thing often happens in homes and churches today.

What motivates an indirect enabler to keep the wall of silence in place?

Motivated by fear and shame

"I just can't talk about it"

When incest occurs within the home, many mothers deny its existence. The book *Surviving the Secret* tells of a study of 112 mothers: "Researchers found that although they denied incest occurring, all the mothers were aware of it and of the collusive role they played."[117] These mothers just wanted to pretend that it didn't happen or that it would just go away. Some may have believed that the crime is so horrendous, so far from the person they thought they were marrying, that they felt as if they couldn't even bring themselves to fully acknowledge the reality.[118] Many of these mothers fear the wrath and anger of the sexual abuser; they fear that things will get worse if they say anything. Sometimes they fear that if the offender is arrested, they may lose the income that they need to live on, even to the point of being homeless. They fear the shame of the stigma that may be attached to their family from that point on.

One lady who told Faith and me her story said that for five years her in-laws had kept her unaware of the abuse her father-in-law had

117   Kathy Rodriguez, Psy.D. and Pam Vredevelt, *Surviving the Secret: Healing the Hurts of Sexual Abuse* (CreateSpace Independent Publishing Platform, 2013), p. 82.

118   A study cited in Crewdson, *By Silence Betrayed*, p. 72, says that as many as 90% of "incest mothers" may have been incest survivors themselves.

perpetrated on one of his grandchildren. He had even pled guilty in court, but she still didn't know. The embarrassment that motivated these family members put young family members at risk.

However accurate any of these fears and shame may be, ultimately these silent enablers are sacrificing another human being on the altar of the fear of man. As we read in Proverbs 29:25, "The fear of man brings a snare." They haven't yet learned the principle of trusting the Lord as is stated in the rest of this verse: "but whoever trusts in the Lord shall be safe."[119] He provides his people with the safety of the spirit, saving us from damnation. This doesn't mean that his people won't suffer, sometimes extremely. But even if we never find justice in the courts of man (and it's not wrong to seek that justice), we can still come out on the other side of suffering victorious, because of the eternal safety of the spirit that we find in his death and resurrection.

A strong and loving church body that is willing to preach against these heinous sins can be a welcoming environment for a mother who is in denial, helping her to tear down the wall of silence, knowing that she will be helped and supported by the community of Christ around her. Besides preaching, the church can make sure that families of abusers know that the church will actively provide practical support if the offender is convicted, similar to what they would provide to a widow or single mother.

---

119   Many sexual abuse survivors still struggle significantly with fear during their journey of healing, because there was a time when their very lives were in danger, and in some cases, they believe that their lives are in danger still. This fear should be taken seriously and dealt with seriously, with compassion and without condemnation.

Motivated by refusal to believe

"It doesn't happen here"

So now Faith's father had pleaded guilty. He got six years' probation and was listed as a registered sex offender. He was supposed to have no contact with children.

But Faith had eight brothers, several of them with children of their own.

Somebody threw a birthday party for somebody. The grandfather was there, the registered sex offender, hugging the children.

How could they stand around with such callous disregard for their children? How could they keep up that wall of silence and turn a blind eye?

I wasn't at the party, but when I heard about it, I called his probation officer and reported it.

There are many in our churches who refuse to listen to the stories of abuse survivors because they simply do not want to believe, first of all, that the men that they thought were "good men" could commit such heinous deeds, and second, that the organizations they trust would ever do something so wrong as to participate in being direct enablers. One time Faith and I spoke with a friend about our ministry and about Faith's story of abuse, when the woman interrupted us. She said, "We don't have this problem in our church."

I was surprised, because years ago I had known a number of people from this woman's church. I thought about the mother who was afraid that her husband was molesting their five-year-old daughter. I thought about the man who used to put up Bible verse signs in his yard—he had raped his daughters. I thought about the grandparents who were concerned that their son-in-law was abusing their grandchildren. I thought about another young lady who had been molested by an older girl. I thought about the young woman, the daughter of a man who had sexually abused his daughters, who was getting married. When someone asked about her dad walking her down the aisle, she said, "No way; I have more respect for a dog than I have for him." The church also supported a mission board that was later found to be fraught with abuse. How could she possibly be so blind as to say, "We don't have this problem in our church"?

The direct enablers, actively covering the abuse, produce the indirect enablers, who because the cover-ups have been successful, truly think their organization is the exception to the statistics. This denial then allows church people to sit back in comfortable ignorance. As the indirect enablers refuse to believe, they play their part in giving offenders more opportunities to harm others.

If we deny a sin's existence, then that very denial becomes an obstacle that must be overcome before we can move on to confession, repentance, and healing. Just as alcoholics must admit that they have a problem before beginning the road to recovery, our churches must admit that we have a serious sexual abuse problem before we can begin the road to overcoming this heinous sin.

Indirect enablers must be willing to open their ears to the cries of the abuse victims or survivors around them. As social media proliferates, the possibility for understanding the truth becomes more and more a reality for anyone who cares enough to find out. Even the bare statistics tell us that approximately 20-25% of the people in our churches are or were abuse victims. So you can't say, "We don't have this problem in our church."

Motivated by indifference and apathy

"It doesn't affect me"

Some who think, "These things just happen, and there's nothing much a person can do about it" may have come to a point of such hopelessness because they were abuse victims themselves.

But there are others who simply don't care. I challenge them to think about Proverbs 31:9, which says, "Open your mouth, judge righteously, and plead the cause of the poor and needy."

Not long ago I received an email from a national family ministry that I greatly respect in response to my request to address the issue of sexual abuse. They said that their ministry has a "well-defined program," and they didn't feel that they were called to deal with this issue. What a tragedy, when they care about families, that they feel they don't need to be bothered with alerting families to the dangers and dealing with the issue of sexual abuse, excusing themselves from responsibility.

As I told a woman about our ministry and the fear some organizations seem to have in addressing it, she soon cut me off, saying, "If it really were God's will for you to do this, the doors would open immediately." This attitude denies the clear and sobering words of Scripture that state when God's people bring truth, often others will not listen.[120]

---

120   God told Jeremiah to prophesy to the people of Judah, but said in Jeremiah 7:27, "Therefore you shall speak all these words to them, but they will not obey you. You shall also call to them, but they will not answer you." He gave Isaiah the negative prophecy, "Go, and say to this people: 'Keep on hearing, but do not understand; keep on seeing, but do not perceive'" (Isaiah 6:9).

By virtue of the silence of these indifferent, apathetic, and distracted people, offenders are able to continue to harm others. This brings about the very embodiment of Edmund Burke's well-known saying, "All that is necessary for evil to triumph is for good men to do nothing."

It's sad when Christian leaders, who could be a cause for righteousness and could influence their congregations to take up the cause of the oppressed, choose rather to absolve themselves of any responsibility to help the abused because they have no interest or are too busy doing other things. This is the time for caring Christians and conscientious churches to become pro-active in these needy areas. This is an opportunity for Christians to take a stand, to support, and be a positive influence for justice. Christian organizations, pastors, missionaries, and countless Christian leaders have a responsibility to help the weak and those who have no voice.

Motivated by an aversion to acknowledging evil

"It's too disturbing to think about"

It's hard, very hard, for many who grew up in good homes and have always been treated well to consider that the Christian world they thought was overall a safe place may actually have some darkness hidden in its midst. It's hard to grasp that evil has happened to people who stand near them in the pews or who used to attend their church. If the topic comes up in small group discussions, they often don't want to hear about it because it's simply too disturbing.

It's clear that doors don't always open for people who are speaking the truth.

An episode of the old *Matlock* television series portrays a man passing through a small western town whose inhabitants seem as if they have something to hide. This newcomer soon realizes that the people are hiding a dark, terrible secret. This can be true in Christian circles as well. At one of our conferences, a woman told us a tragic story of a dark secret. She had married an older man who seemed to be a wonderful Christian. He had an adult daughter, now married, whom he had raised for many years after her mother had died. His family members seemed to be nice Christians, but the fact was that they were all hiding a very ugly secret. Once the woman married this man and moved into her new husband's house, she began to realize that something was terribly wrong. Her new husband's daughter spent more time with her father than with her own husband, time in a private bedroom early in the morning. Then, at least twelve people—family, friends, and even acquaintances—expressed their concern over her new husband's relationship with his daughter. Nobody had done anything, though, so this new wife, who had believed she had married a godly man, had walked into a nightmare, with an adult daughter who may well have been trained to believe that she had no choice except to do her father's wishes.

Perhaps the possibility that this man really was raping his daughter throughout her growing-up years was just too terrible for people to think about, much less act on. Their aversion to evil kept them silent about something that should not have been kept silent.

Silence in the face of the evil of sexual abuse continues to allow the evil to go on and on, unabated. We've heard of cases in the news in which someone is being robbed and passersby do nothing. We're horrified that nobody would get involved, that nobody would stop the robbery, nobody would help the victim. But the same thing is happening all around us with sexual abuse.

It's a difficult subject to tackle, but compassionate people in our churches need to take it on. Our churches must become more willing to expose sexual perpetrators and offer compassionate help to those who have been violated. The time of avoiding and looking the other way must come to an end. This is a spiritual battle that must be fought.

A serious question arises: How many precious innocent souls will we allow to be sacrificed on the altar of fear and aversion before we stand up and become the people that God has called us to be?

WHAT GOD SAYS ABOUT ENABLERS

The dynamic of enablers is never so clear-cut as to be placed into just one of the categories above. Usually the motivation behind covering abuse and blaming and shaming victims is a complicated mess of several or even most of the factors mentioned. Entire books have been written to try to analyze the cognitive dissonance that is overcome by willful blindness.[121] But though enablers rarely stop to analyze the reason for their enabling, the condemnation they fall under is the same.

As Solomon viewed his world, he saw a great deal of injustice. He said in Ecclesiastes 3:16, "I saw under the sun: in the place of judgment,

---

121   One book that is especially helpful in this arena is *Willful Blindness: Why We Ignore the Obvious at Our Peril* by Margaret Heffernan (New York: Walker & Company, 2012). Heffernan analyzes the factors that create willful blindness, observing that within a proscribed culture, the pressure to conform often holds sway. This concept especially applies in microcosmic cultures such as isolated church environments in which everyone is expected to conform to a very specific set of rules, including the rule of no-speak, under the guise of "gossip is sin." On page 27 Heffernan says, "Under social pressure, most of us would simply rather be wrong than alone."

wickedness was there; and in the place of righteousness, iniquity was there." This is a great tragedy. Could it be that this tragedy is taking place in our very own churches?

When the Israelite people were at the worst time morally in their history, ripe for judgment, God said in Jeremiah 7:30–31, "They have set their abominations in the house which is called by my name, to pollute it . . . to burn their sons and their daughters in the fire, which I did not command, nor did it come into my heart." How different is the behavior of many churches today than the Jews in the days of Jeremiah? Every time a church looks the other way or refuses to protect the vulnerable ones that God has sent to them, they are little different than those who sacrificed their children in the fire. In Luke 12:2 our Lord Jesus Christ spoke these ominous words: "For there is nothing covered that will not be revealed, nor hidden that will not be known." And Numbers 32:23 reminds us, "Be sure your sin will find you out."

Jesus said in Matthew 24:12 that there would come a day when "the love of many will grow cold." Enablers may have many reasons for protecting offenders, but none of them are about genuine love. Will Christians continue to simply pass by the victims of abuse, as did the priest and the Levite who passed by the man who was wounded on the road and left for dead?[122] If our churches don't seriously respond to this epidemic, we'll have no credibility, no power, and no words of hope to reach those who are in darkness.

In 2 Kings 5, Elisha's servant Gehazi had just accepted some gifts he was told not to accept. When confronted, he chose to deny what he had done. This denial cost him dearly—it cost him a chance to confess,

---

122   This is a reference to the parable of the Good Samaritan, found in Luke 10:25–37.

a chance to repent, a chance for forgiveness and mercy. The disease of leprosy that came into his body was even passed down through his family for generations. When church leaders choose to deny that sexual abuse is occurring, they are, in effect, bringing on themselves and their churches the "leprosy" of this heinous sin and all the suffering that goes with it. These consequences may go on for generations.

In Proverbs 17:15 Solomon says, "He who justifies the wicked, and he who condemns the just, both of them alike are an abomination to the Lord." The enabling of the offender that helps him escape the consequences of his sin is an abomination to the Lord. The condemnation of the innocent, claiming that sexual assault was the victim's fault is an abomination to the Lord. God's Word is clear.

When people of a church ignore a traumatizing crime, the trauma is exponentially increased. When victims are left without remedy because the local church chooses to avoid its responsibility in dealing with this huge issue, the church is declaring itself ripe for judgment. "Woe to those," says Isaiah 5:20, "who call evil good, and good evil; who put darkness for light, and light for darkness; who put bitter for sweet, and sweet for bitter!" Our prayer is that Christians will believe and speak the truth, recognizing how damaging sexual abuse is and how it harms individuals and families.

A PLEA FROM A SEXUAL ABUSE SURVIVOR

It seems fitting to end this chapter with a message from a sexual abuse survivor, written to those in Christian ministry who, for a variety of reasons, want to cover the crime of sexual abuse.

Consider this: What if I witnessed my child killed by a drunk driver in my front yard? What if I held my child, realizing that he is dead, saw the driver exit her car stumbling around in an obvious state of drunkenness, saw her car filled with bottles of alcohol partially emptied?

Would I need to remain silent? Could I share my agony, confusion, and suffering with my church family or the community at large? Or would I be told to remain silent because the autopsy has not yet been completed and the driver who has admitted to being drunk has not yet been sentenced in court?

What if the drunk driver is declared incompetent to stand trial due to some extenuating circumstances? Does that make it any less true that she has killed my child and I am hurting? What if she is a respected leader in the community? Should I hide my pain to protect her? What if she is a Sunday school teacher, well-loved within our own church family? Does that mean I must remain completely silent and alone in order to not add to her pain?

What if I have forgiven her and have compassion for the struggle she is facing? Does that mean I can't struggle and be open about my own pain as well?[123]

When people refuse to help someone who has been abused, they are in effect saying that this valuable soul is valueless.

For the love of Christ, for the love of those who have been torn apart by sexual abuse, we cannot remain silent.

---

123   Personal correspondence, used by permission.

PART TWO

STOP THE WRONG THINKING

BELIEVE AND SPEAK THE TRUTH

CHAPTER 6

TEAR DOWN THIS WALL OF WRONG THINKING

JUST DON'T TALK ABOUT IT?

For over twenty years of marriage, Faith and I had sometimes discussed the issue of her abuse, but only in an indirect sort of way. I still didn't know exactly what it was that had happened to her. I hadn't wanted to know details—it was just too ugly. And Faith hadn't seemed to want to talk about it.

But now, in 2005 in our small church, her father had confessed to molesting his foster granddaughter. Now it was coming out that there had been other victims.

Now, no matter how painful it was, I had to know the truth.

We sat together, and I held her hand. She knew I needed to know.

"Faith," I asked gently, "what was it your father did to you, exactly?"

She was silent, struggling, trying to find the words. I offered one.

"Did he rape you?"

She looked down. "Yes."

"How old were you?"

"I was nine . . . when it started."

"When it started? What do you mean? How long did it go on?"

"For almost nine years. Till just shortly before I went to college."

Over eight years? And all these years I hadn't known?

Young people at Christian colleges need to know that they can speak about these dark issues and get the help they need as they try to work through matters that will affect them for the rest of their lives. But in far too many of them, the wall of silence remains. Our own alma mater, now Davis College, has been a notable exception, having enthusiastically invited our Speaking Truth in Love Ministries to the campus, but in the majority of Christian colleges, the wall of silence remains. "Thank you anyway, but we don't need your help," responded one college when we wrote offering to speak there in 2006. "We're afraid our students will focus on the issue if we talk about it," replied two others. Almost fifty other Christian colleges we wrote to replied with . . . silence.

Commonly, if Christian ministries allow any discussion about sexual abuse at all, they would prefer for it only to refer to the abuse survivor's forgiveness and healing, without mentioning the criminal offender. This positive side of the story is usually acceptable to them, but to talk about the darkness of the sin and the truth about offenders—their devious hypocrisy and even charm, their lying, manipulating ways, the steps they take to groom and silence their victims—and the need to hold them accountable for their sin, for some reason is often not acceptable.

Over the years we've corresponded with many pastors, missionaries, Christian radio stations, and Christian cable channels in an effort to bring attention to this sin. Many churches respond to us by saying that they do background checks on those who work in their children's ministries. This is good, but it won't stop the offenders who haven't yet been caught, and it won't heal the church members who are struggling with abuse from their past.

Christians in places of leadership and influence often seem to think that they don't need to talk about sexual assault in an intentionally public way. But they do. They need to warn and prepare others for what is ultimately a spiritual battle. They need to tear down this wall of silence.

"WE DON'T WANT TO HURT THE CAUSE OF CHRIST"

A common concern felt by many well-meaning Christians is the fear that admitting that there's a problem with such a heinous crime within our churches will hurt the efforts of the churches or ministries, who are trying to lead people to Christ. Faith and I have heard this concern expressed many times, at conferences and churches where we've spoken, and in other venues.

My response to that is: *Have we absolutely lost our minds?* It is the *sin* that hurts the work of Christ and brings shame to the church— not exposing it! Not telling the truth about it! Not actually dealing with it! How can dealing with abuse and holding offenders accountable for their sins possibly hurt the name of Christ?

Ephesians 5:11–12 reminds Christians, "Have no fellowship with the unfruitful works of darkness, but rather expose them. For it is shameful even to speak of those things which are done by them in secret." We are commanded by God to expose evil. Why would God tell people to "expose" the works of darkness, if doing so would hurt His work? Some have said that because these things are shameful to speak about, abuse victims should keep silent about their abuse. This is far from the case! The Bible is full of discussions of shameful sins, but always with a redemptive motive, showing the terrible end of the shameful works of darkness. Paul isn't saying in one verse that we should reprove the works of darkness and then in another verse that we shouldn't talk about them. Rather, he is telling us to reprove them with a redemptive purpose. If there is ever a biblical mandate for dealing with this sin, it's here in these verses.

If a church fails to expose the truth about abuse and biblically deal with it, then it's safe to conclude that there is little or no light in that church. Christians need to be aware of the wrong beliefs and fears that get in the way of making right decisions when it comes to this issue. They need to be informed, to be vigilant, and to take appropriate action when needed.

God's will is that these works of darkness need to be exposed. It is the light of truth that exposes the evil. This is one of the very best ways possible to help the cause of Christ.

TEAR DOWN THIS WALL OF PRIDE

A return to ancient Corinth?

Often Christians can see the sin in other churches or in other de-nominations, but pride keeps them from seeing the sin in their own, blinding them to the truth. In 1 Corinthians 5:1–2 Paul says, "It is ac-tually reported that there is sexual immorality among you, and such sexual immorality as is not even named among the Gentile—that a man has his father's wife! And *you are puffed up,* and have not rather mourned, that he who has done this deed might be taken away from among you" (Italics added).

Corinth was a very immoral culture, but in this case even the pagans were astonished with this brazen lifestyle. Paul didn't focus so much on the man as on the church and their puffed-up indiffer-ence to a lifestyle that shocked even the unbelievers. Because their pride had allowed this evil to be practiced and the offender went unchecked and unconfronted, the pagan lifestyles all around them paled in comparison.

But notice the reason they hadn't mourned and taken action against this sin. It was because of their arrogance.

When they are arrogant, Christians are unable to mourn over sin. But the need is great for the church to mourn for the victims who have lost their innocence, lost their joy and sense of self-worth, lost their ability to love and trust, and, in many cases, lost their reason for living. The need is great for churches to mourn over their own callousness and resistance to taking this egregious sin seriously, their own willingness to cover for the perpetrators.

Not long ago, Faith talked with a lady whose daughter had been molested by a person at her church. When this lady asked her pastor about bringing one of these abuse awareness ministries into their church, he said he wouldn't, because "it's too complex of a situation, and no one else outside of our church would understand." This pastor's pride kept him from helping his church deal with the abuse that had harmed their very own children.

This pastor's reaction is typical. Similar scenarios play out time and time again in churches throughout our country. The pride of our church leaders keeps many of them from tearing down the wall of silence and secrecy, refusing to allow those trained and skilled in this issue to help them understand how to more effectively deal with it. The sin of the offenders causes the initial damage, but the pride of many of our church leaders keeps this sin alive and well.

In our ministry we hear frequently from well-meaning Christians that we are not supposed to judge. The "no-judging" mantra was exactly what was happening in the Corinthian church in 1 Corinthians 5. And yet in verses 11–12, God makes it very clear that we are to judge those who are within the church. If Paul were here today, he would give a scathing report on many churches that resist taking action in the name of "not judging," when they could be pro-active about the evil in their churches.

When Solomon was about to be crowned king of Israel, he asked for the ability to "judge," or discern, between good and evil. In Proverbs 31:9, he admonished us, "Open your mouth, judge righteously, and plead the cause of the poor and needy."

"Judging righteously" is discerning between good and evil. How many of us are asking God to have hearts that can discern between good and evil? What will be the result of that discernment when He grants it? Proverbs 31:9 gives us the answer.

Tear down this wall on your knees

The antidote to pride is humility and mourning over sin. Pastors and all Christians should be on their knees before God with tears in their eyes and a broken heart, pleading with God for forgiveness and for the wisdom to help minister to those who are hurting from abuse, trusting Him for the strength to hold offenders accountable.

Even though the gospel of Christ may be an offense to many, we're not to be an offense ourselves by hypocrisy. The day must come when the whole body of Christ awakes and sees this sin for what it is, as I did in 2005. I pray that we will all be truly sickened by it and fall on our knees in mourning, repentance, and confession to God for not dealing with it years ago.

Lest you're tempted to say that you don't need to mourn and confess because you haven't been a part of this sin, don't forget that when Daniel prayed in Daniel chapter 9, he confessed the sin of Israel and included himself, as he asked God for forgiveness.

TEAR DOWN THIS WALL OF DENIAL

It's difficult to grasp the fact that the evil of sexual abuse exists in our midst. It's even more difficult to accept the fact that it is prevalent.

There is no conscionable way that we can deny, excuse, or minimize this sin, yet because it is so troubling to believe that this is happening in the body of Christ, many are willing to do just that in order to ease their consciences. As a result, when Christians are faced with the realization that people within our churches are guilty of these horrible offenses, the first response is often disbelief and denial. Christians don't want to believe that such a thing can happen in our midst, so many will convince themselves that it just doesn't. As a result, victims are further intimidated into silence because they fear no one will believe them, while the sin continues to devastate the lives of those who attend their churches.

One woman reported that when she was being abused as a young person, she could look out the window and see the church where she would walk with her family the next day, sometimes barely able to hobble because of the extent of the abuse. But they had to hurry, because her abuser needed to get there in time to sing in the choir. There the people would give exuberant testimony about their love for Jesus and their love for each other and the presence of the Lord in their meetings.

Sometimes the abuse even happens within the church building itself. A young woman said that she had been molested for years in a Sunday school room during the church service. I wonder what God must have felt as the people in the sanctuary prayed for Him to bless them and fill the church and prosper their ministry, while sexual abuse was going on in a nearby room.

Christians must resist the temptation to take comfort in the fact that they didn't know about a particular instance of abuse. Even if sin is hidden, it still has consequences. Proverbs 21:3 says, "To do righteousness and justice is more acceptable to the Lord than sacrifice." The consequences of this sin, this crime, are so serious and tragic that nothing that could ever be presented should allow an abuser or the church to minimize it. Excusing sexual abuse is neither loving nor forgiving. Christians must stop making excuses and start holding offenders accountable. The wall of denial must be torn down.

STOP TRYING TO PROTECT THE CHURCH FROM SCANDAL

"Dale, I have to say, I'm disappointed in you."

I'd been hearing a lot of emotional responses from my church members ever since we'd contacted the police about my father-in-law's crime.

"Oh, why is that, Mr. Davidson?" Mr. Davidson was in his nineties and had been a deacon forever.

"Don't you know that the church ought to deal with our own problems in house? We shouldn't be calling those outsiders in. It's a shameful thing for the world to see our problems. It's our job to take care of it, just like it says in Second Corinthians 6, you know, why can't you deal with your own issues yourself."

"But Mr. Davidson—"

"Listen, Dale, I've been around way longer than you have. Years ago, when you were probably just a boy, I had a friend who did something with a girl—not much different from what's happened here. Our church handled it. We never had to call the law."

I grimaced inwardly. "How did your church handle it?"

"Oh, we talked with him. He saw the light about what he did."

"And then what?"

"Well, he moved away. Lost track of him. But everything was kept quiet. No scandal like what we're dealing with here."

He moved away . . . to continue his evil crimes without anyone ever knowing.

In 2010 when the British Petroleum oil spill disaster killed eleven people and contaminated the Gulf of Mexico with millions of gallons of oil, the CEO Tony Hayward caused outrage when he selfishly said, "I'd like my life back."[124] When the church tells someone whose life has been so damaged by sexual abuse that they can't report this crime or even speak about the matter, they are sending the same message: "You don't matter, your pain doesn't matter, and the injustice doesn't matter. We just want our life and ministry to be undisturbed."

Many churches will welcome attorneys who offer training, as long as it helps them prevent a lawsuit. The picture that this behavior seems to paint is that many church cultures seem more concerned about money issues than they are about whether or not sexual violations of precious souls are occurring on their watch. An attorney told us that he admonishes organizations to deal fully with any report of abuse, but he added that in most cases ministry leaders would give in to the mistaken belief that if they could only hide or suppress the reports, that there would be less damage to the organization. But the attorney confirmed that, consistently, it was always the opposite. When people choose to deny and try to cover up an allegation of sexual assault—which, if it involves children, is in itself a crime—instead of facing a scandal about one individual, they may ultimately have to

---

124   Jessica Durando, "BP's Tony Hayward: 'I'd like my life back,'" USA Today, June 1, 2010, accessed at http://content.usatoday.com/communities/greenhouse/post/2010/06/bp-tony-hayward-apology/1#.VEmOhtJoyM8.

face a scandal about a cover-up perpetrated by an entire organization. The Penn State scandal that came to light in the fall of 2011 serves as an example. The continued cover-up of Sandusky's child sexual assaults ultimately resulted not only in far more victims but in national scandal for the entire university.[125]

Shortly after the news broke about the scandal at Penn State, stories began to surface about several other Christian organizations that had been covering up abuse for years. The public image of these organizations had taken many years to build, but the fallout from covering abuse has served to tarnish their reputations.

Recently we've been working with some believers whose pastor molested a teenage girl in their church. When the church turned to their denomination leadership for help, they did send a representative to come and talk with them about abuse. After going through some brief training and telling the church how to protect themselves from a lawsuit, they felt that they had sufficiently dealt with the situation. There was no attempt to deal with the larger spiritual issues, to help the victim, to pay for counseling, or to reach out to the parents. The whole focus was to get the situation behind them as quickly as possible.

So what are the church leaders really saying who refuse to deal with this issue? That maybe it's okay after all for the powerful to sexually violate the powerless? No one would ever say that, but that's exactly the perception they're conveying.

According to 1 Corinthians 13, if we accomplish "great" things, but have no love, we are accomplishing nothing. If God withdraws His

---

125   Sylvia L. Kurtz, *To Believe a Kid: Understanding the Jerry Sandusky Case and Child Sexual Abuse* (Xlibris, 2014).

blessing because of the covering of sin, all the money in the world can't build a church or Christian ministry that will accomplish anything of lasting value. If our churches will effectively deal with the issue of sexual abuse, even though it will take time and effort, this will be an important step in restoring God's blessing.

What will God have to do to bring the church to its knees?

STOP SUBVERTING JUSTICE

The church body needs to realize and remember that the sin of sexual abuse is also a criminal offense; therefore we have a moral, logical, and legal obligation to treat it as such. Romans 13:3–5 says, "For rulers are not a terror to good works, but to evil. Do you want to be unafraid of the authority? Do what is good, and you will have praise from the same. For he is God's minister to you for good. But if you do evil, be afraid; for he does not bear the sword in vain; for he is God's minister, an avenger to execute wrath on him who practices evil. Therefore you must be subject, not only because of wrath but also for conscience' sake."

For some reason, though people are able to recognize the need for justice with other criminal activities such as murder, assault, or theft, many conclude that somehow in this case, justice is wrong.[126] But we must hold offenders accountable before God and the law.

When the child molestation committed by Faith's father became public, we held him accountable, turned him over to the police, and eventually excommunicated him. Though some of the people in our church made excuses for him and left the church, the majority of

---

126   These misunderstandings are dealt with more fully in chapter 9, "Believe and Speak the Truth about Mercy and Justice, Grace and Love."

our church has been very supportive, supporting Faith and me as we started Speaking Truth in Love Ministries to speak out against sexual abuse in the Christian community.

But this level of support is rare. In our churches and Christian organizations, offenders are being protected and the ones they victimized are being pushed aside for the sake of the institution. Until we take these steps to tear down the wall that has been built up over the years to protect this sin, God's judgment will be swift and severe, and it will start in His house.

CHAPTER 7

BELIEVE AND SPEAK THE TRUTH ABOUT SIN AND ITS CONSEQUENCES

ARE ALL SINS REALLY EQUAL?

I have heard many Christians say things like "One sin is as bad as another" or "Sin is sin." I cringe each time I hear this. Religious sexual offenders love to use these ideas as a way to try to lessen the degree of their sin and to try to make themselves seem like average Christians with a few bad habits.

The idea that all sins are equal is a relatively new one, apparently having arisen within the last hundred years, and mistakenly spun off of Jesus' words in Matthew 5, such as verse 28, which says, "But I say to you that whoever looks at a woman to lust for her has already committed adultery with her in his heart."

Jesus said lusting was heart adultery. So then, many extrapolate, it must be that lusting after a woman is just as bad as committing unspeakable atrocities against her. But then . . . you have to draw the corollary. That means that committing unspeakable atrocities against a woman is no worse than lusting after her in your heart.

Really?

While it is true that all sin is bad and is a violation of God's law, there clearly are degrees of sin. They're shown in the punishments for various sins and the progression of sin.

Making the punishments fit the crimes

In the Old Testament, when God gave His law to the children of Israel, He assigned different punishments for different sins. Leviticus 6:2–5 says that in the case of robbery or extortion, the punishment was the restoration of the full value plus one fifth. But Exodus 21:16 says that the punishment for kidnapping was death. If the sins were simply equal, the punishment would also be the same. In both cases, the sin is a violation of God's law, but God assures that the punishment fit the crime.

In Ezekiel 16:52 God said to the nation of Judah, "You who judged your sisters, bear your own shame also, because the sins which you committed were more abominable than theirs." Is there a difference that makes sin more abominable than another? According to God's Word there absolutely is.

Ezekiel chapter 8 shows God taking the prophet to see "greater" and "greater" abominations, each one worse than the last. In 1 Corinthians 5 Paul told the Corinthians that the sin they had in their church was worse than the sin of the unsaved. Obviously God holds some sins to be worse than others.

Luke 12:47–48a says, "And that servant who knew his master's will, and did not prepare himself or do according to his will, shall be beaten with many stripes. But he who did not know, yet committed things deserving of stripes, shall be beaten with few."

All sin is wrong, but according to God's Word some sin is more egregious than others, demanding different severities of punishment for the different severities of sin. Lying or stealing is a sin, but the rape of a precious child is a worse sin. And shame on those who cannot acknowledge that biblical truth. Any thinking Christian who understands the issues knows that it is heinous to rape and abuse a vulnerable person, and there can be no doubt as to God's anger and wrath at such an evil act. The punishment for this crime indeed will be most severe.

Sin progresses from bad to worse

Sin that is not confessed and dealt with will always grow worse and worse. Here's how it works out practically:

Do you find yourself attracted to and seduced by an evil thought? Then repent on the spot, right then. Turn to Christ.

But do you go a step further and let that thought work out into action? Then repent right then, not only before God, but before the one your action affected.

But do you go a step further and let that action work out into practice? Repent and turn to Christ. Receive His forgiveness and His power to overcome that sin. Make humble, penitent restitution in whatever way is necessary to anyone who has been affected by your sin.

But do you go a step further—or many, many steps—and seek to shroud that practice behind a cloak of manmade-rule-keeping respectability that becomes more and more elaborate to cover your terrible secrets, as you preach louder and longer and make more complicated and burdensome rules and hold conferences and write books *decrying the very sins that you yourself are secretly practicing?*

Then woe unto you, hypocrite, blind fool! You're shutting up the kingdom of heaven against men. You will not go in yourself, just as you're blocking the door for those who want to enter. You will receive the greater judgment.[127]

Are you causing young believers to stumble and go astray, and in some cases to leave the faith entirely? Then it would be better for you if a millstone were hanged around your neck and you were cast into the depths of the sea.

Do you find that "looking good" is more important than dealing with sin in your midst, lest you lose your image of outward perfection? Then you're cleaning the outside of the cup, but the inside is full of extortion and excess. Serpents, generation of vipers!

Are you willing for someone to confront you with wrong, even about something major? Are you willing to receive it, repent, and make it right, even publicly if necessary? If you are, then, as when Nathan came to David, you can be received and forgiven.

But if you're not, then every disciple you work so hard to make will become twofold more a child of hell than yourself.

---

127   This is an echo of Jesus' words in Matthew 23. We have seen men who cry out for judgment against sinners who themselves are practicing heinous sins.

Sin is always progressive; if it isn't confessed and repented of, it will grow worse and worse, to the point where it will destroy a person or a church or even a society.

DON'T MITIGATE THE CONSEQUENCES

Proverbs 28:17 says, "A man burdened with bloodshed will flee into a pit; *let no one help him*." The first time I read this verse, I was surprised, because it seemed as if God were being unfair or harsh to tell people not to help. But this verse has a powerful message for the church about dealing with sexual offenders. We can pray for them and share the gospel with them, but we are not to try to break their fall or ease the consequences of their bloodshed in any way.

One of the most important ways that children learn the difference between right and wrong is by experiencing the consequences of their actions and by observing others experience the consequences of their actions. When the church refuses to hold sexual offenders accountable but instead insulates them from the consequences, the offenders receive the clear message that they can commit these crimes and get away with them. Unfortunately, the tragic facts are that statistically, few offenders ever truly change, even those who make a full confession and appear truly repentant. Everyone must always be on guard against the perpetrator's tendencies to rape or molest the vulnerable. If there is any hope of change or reform, it will usually be tied to the consequences of their sin. Our churches need for all of us to come together and be united in holding predators accountable for their crimes.

Even if they are never reported to the police,[128] even if they are reported but get off with a light sentence or found not guilty, offenders need to feel the full force of the consequences of what they have done.[129] When church leaders intervene to protect an accused predator and try to keep him from the police or get him off with an easy sentence, they are helping to prolong his reign of abuse. They embolden him to go even further with his abuse because he has been able to get away with it.

Lest you harm the offender

When church people protect an offender, they are actually harming him—they mistakenly remove a necessary warning sign of God's impending judgment. The problem is similar to dealing with someone with a drinking problem. Some families try to do everything they can to protect an alcoholic from the consequences of what he has done and is doing, but before you know it, he's behind the wheel again endangering the public, and may wind up in jail. How much did this protective behavior really help?

Psalm 107:17 reminds us, "Fools, because of their transgression, and because of their iniquities, were afflicted." Experiencing the appropriate consequences of their actions is one God-given way for

---

128   There are several reasons why an offender may never be reported to the police. Though statute of limitations laws are changing for the better in many states, there are still cases in which offenses happened too long ago to report. Also, though abuse perpetrated on a minor is a mandated reporting event, adult victims may choose not to report the crimes perpetrated on them for their own reasons. Victims should never be pressured to report, but should be encouraged that if they choose to do so, they'll have a loving support system in place to walk with them through the grueling experience of the court system.

129   A process for carrying through in a Christ-like way with church consequences for the offender is delineated in Chapter 11, "What the Offender Must Do."

evildoers to reconsider their ways, meditate on the coming judgment of God, and cry out to Him for a change of heart.

Lest you hinder God's just judgment

It is appropriate that calamities befall a sexual offender as a result of his evil behavior, just as it is appropriate that calamities should befall a devious murderer. If he loses his ministry, his family, the fellowship of other believers, these consequences are appropriate, and he should not be protected from them. When people interfere with the consequences of a sexual offender's sin, they interfere with God's plan to deal with the sin.

Lest you send the wrong message to the ones who are watching

Proverbs 22:5 paints a clear picture when it states, "Thorns and snares are in the way of the perverse; he who guards his soul will be far from them." A wise person will keep a careful distance from the offender. If the church tries to minimize the crime and protect the perpetrator, the younger followers won't understand the need to guard themselves and their children against such evildoers, and others may come to believe they too can engage in atrocious crimes without immediate consequences. Will Christians heed God's warnings?

Think of all the people in the Bible who experienced the consequences of their actions. In Acts 5, Ananias and Sapphira were struck dead by God for lying to the Holy Spirit. Moses, even though he was a great man of God, was not allowed to go into the Promised Land because he had disobeyed God on one occasion. If God refused to exempt Moses from the consequences of his actions, what does God think of those professing Christians who do everything possible to keep sexual offenders from going to jail?

In Matthew 18:6–8, Jesus gave a warning to offenders:

> Whoever causes one of these little ones who believes in me to sin, it would be better for him if a millstone were hung around his neck, and he were drowned in the depth of the sea. Woe to the world because of offenses! For offenses must come, but woe to that man by whom the offense comes! If your hand or foot causes you to sin, cut it off and cast it from you. It is better for you to enter into life lame or maimed, rather than having two hands or two feet, to be cast into the everlasting fire.

What did Jesus mean when he said these troubling words? Someone who offends a child is in danger of going to hell, and if severing a part of your body will help keep you from offending a child, than you would be better off with an incomplete body than to spend eternity in hell.

Consequences can be very severe, but they are mandated in the Scriptures as a way to both deal with sin and be a deterrent from sin. Offenders have good reason to be afraid when they hear what God has to say about them. If you love the offender, don't protect him from the consequences of his actions, as you may be the one helping to push him through the gates of hell. If you love him, tell him the truth about what God's Word has to say—maybe he will be terrified enough to truly confess and truly repent.

CHAPTER 8

BELIEVE AND SPEAK THE TRUTH ABOUT FORGIVENESS

For some reason, when it comes to sexual abuse, Christians often misunderstand the biblical teaching on forgiveness. This misunderstanding contributes to the flawed environment that allows offenders to sneak in and prey on the vulnerable and get away with it time and time again.

SHOULD WE JUST . . . OVERLOOK IT?

"It was my father."

We sat together on the bench outside the dorm, twenty-two-year-old seniors in Bible college, working through an issue alone that young people should never have to work through alone.

Faith was gazing out, at nothing, rather than looking at me.

The woman I loved and wanted to marry had been violated by the very man who was supposed to have protected her the most. I was in shock, and numb.

But then anger rose to the surface. I clenched my fists, and my stomach churned. I felt like throwing up. I was so angry I didn't know what to do.

"I never want to have anything to do with him, ever again," I muttered. "I never want to see him again."

Faith sighed. It was hard for her, so hard. But she loved the Lord and wanted to do right.

"The Bible says we're supposed to forgive," she said.

What could I do? As angry as I was, I knew she was right. The Bible says we're supposed to forgive. And I loved the Lord too. I wanted to do right too.

In my youth and ignorance, I never thought about the implications of just overlooking the sin. It didn't even occur to me that there may well have been other victims. It never crossed my mind that what he had done was a crime, not just against Faith, but against society, and should have been reported to the police. I didn't even think to ask if he had ever repented. I didn't understand the "ifs" of Scripture—"if he confesses," and "if he repents." In our naiveté, we both thought of forgiveness as something that had to be extended unconditionally.

The numbness that was so familiar to Faith set in for me. Ten months later, Faith and I stood at the altar together. The man conducting the wedding ceremony . . . was the man we had "forgiven."

What we had done was not forgiveness at all; it was simply doing nothing.

We just didn't know.

Since the church in America has an abysmal record for holding sexual offenders accountable for the crimes they commit, it seems that the vast majority of Christians in our country must have the same mistaken impression about the meaning of forgiveness that we had as twenty-two-year-olds.

HOW DOES GOD'S FORGIVENESS WORK?

In the New Testament, the idea conveyed about forgiveness is that if someone sins against another and then confesses and repents and seeks forgiveness, the one who has been sinned against will release him from any personal desire for vengeance or repayment. As Christians, we see that the basis for all forgiveness is what Jesus Christ has accomplished for all of us on the cross.

Every person alive desperately needs God's forgiveness. Romans 3:23 says, "For all have sinned and fall short of the glory of God." The good news in 2 Corinthians 5:21 says, "For he made him who knew no sin to be sin for us, that we might become the righteousness of God in him." Christ's sacrifice was sufficient to pay for any and all sin.

But every true Christian knows that even though Christ died for the sins of the world, forgiveness is not given automatically to anyone. If it were, everyone would be saved without the need to cry out to Christ. Forgiveness counts for each of us only when we ask God for it through the sacrifice and victory of Jesus Christ, when we put our faith and trust in Christ alone, agreeing with God about our sinful state (confession) and coming to our senses about the wrong road we've chosen and the right road He offers (repentance). Anyone who claims right standing with God without doing these things is deceiving himself.

TRUE CONFESSION, TRUE REPENTANCE

November of 2005, when my father-in-law was caught molesting a young teenage girl, the wall of silence in our family toppled. Faith wrote letters making sure everyone in the family knew what had happened to her as a child.

Her father wrote a letter of his own to Faith. "What you said is true, and I'm sorry," he wrote. He spoke to his son on the phone, the foster father of the girl he had molested. "I'm sorry," he said. (We were still so naïve, hoping that he was moving on the road to true repentance. Behind our backs, we found out later, he was giving a different story to the people of the church.)

One night on the phone weeks later, one of Faith's brothers was trying again to confront his father with his sin.

Her father whined, "I said I was sorry. What more can I do?"

We made it clear what more he could do.[130] Because saying you're sorry is—like the pseudo-forgiveness we offered as young people—basically doing nothing at all.

We had wanted to see fruits of repentance. Instead, he continued to talk about how he was being persecuted, and he bragged about how great it was that he was a Christian and going to heaven and death was no big deal.

---

130   A substantive and meaningful response for the offender is addressed in Chapter 11, "What the Offender Must Do."

We had required that he turn himself in. Instead, he got a lawyer.

"Find all your victims and ask them for forgiveness and make restitution," we said. He countered with, "What if I can't remember them all?"

I could barely even comprehend his arrogance. Did he ever once consider the devastation his crimes had wrought? Did he ever once consider falling on his face before God in shame and crying out to him?

If he once got a glimpse of the anger of God against him for his offenses, his knees would be too weak to stand.

First John 1:9 says, "If we confess our sins, He is faithful and just to forgive us our sins." Biblical *confession* means "agreeing with God about the sin." Only when we confess—agree with God about our sin—does God extend forgiveness to us.

The truth about forgiveness is that the first responsibility is laid on the one who sinned to make a true confession—without excuses. He must be willing to see his sin as God sees it, which means being willing to look at all of the darkness and destruction of his past.

Though no one can fake true confession before God, an offender can mimic a confession that seems credible before other people. Many offenders, when they see that they've been caught, are able to manufacture tears at a moment's notice and express great contrition. Especially because the offender is so often "such a nice man," many in our churches will want to quickly receive this confession and move forward with forgiveness and reinstatement.

But not so fast. How can we as discerning believers recognize whether or not that confession is credible?

In Luke 3:7-8a, John warned the Jews, "Brood of vipers! Who warned you to flee from the wrath to come? Therefore bear fruits worthy of repentance." The Greek word translated *repent* means "to turn from going one direction and go the other direction." Inherent in the definition is the understanding that the one who is turning has realized that he was going the wrong way, essentially, that he has come to his senses, as the prodigal son did when he made the decision to return to his father's house.[131] This term "fruits worthy of repentance" makes it clear that repentance is not simply weeping tears of remorse that may or may not be genuine, but is borne out in an entire life lived in a new direction. These fruits of true repentance will include a willingness to bear the consequences of his sin.[132]

In *Surviving the Secret,* the authors say, "Absolute, pure forgiveness can be granted only when repentance is extended."[133] If a true Christian is stubborn, refusing to truly confess and truly repent, then according to Hebrews 12 he will be chastened by God, and if he continues to harden his heart, it may even result in death. The sexual offender is no exception: unless he makes a true confession with true repentance, his sin remains unforgiven.

The book *Laura* tells the story of a young girl whose father prostituted her.[134] One of the men who routinely paid to rape her was a

---

131 This story is found in Luke 15:11–32.

132 See Chapter 11, "What the Offender Must Do."

133 Rodriguez and Vredevelt, *Surviving the Secret,* p. 129.

134 Alaine Pakkala, *Laura: A True Story* (Camp Hill, PA: Christian Publications, 2002).

preacher who continued to preach to his congregation every Sunday. Each time he raped her, he spoke words asking God to forgive him. Did God forgive this evil man simply because he spoke words as if he were asking for forgiveness in order to avoid the penalty of his sin? This man surely knew that what he was doing was terribly wrong, but he refused to acknowledge his sin as the enormity it was. He didn't see himself the way God saw him, without the mask. He never experienced true confession, agreeing with God about his sin. He never confessed his crime to authorities. He never showed true repentance, turning from this evil way and purposefully going the other way.

According to the meanings of true confession and true repentance in the Scriptures, we must conclude that he was not forgiven.

GRANTING FORGIVENESS

Anger is sometimes used as a shield against fear. Refusing to forgive in some cases says to an offender, "I'm taking your crime against me very seriously." Forgiveness, on the other hand, is an opening of the hands to release a debtor from his enormous debt. Depending on the enormity of the offense and the vulnerability of the one who was offended against, true forgiveness may be a very long and difficult road. The ability to grant forgiveness to one who has inflicted great destruction in the life is a gift from God—to know that the crime was a very serious one, and yet at the same time to be willing to open the hands to release the debtor from the debt.

We hear too many stories of church leaders bringing the abuse survivor into the same room with the offender, where the offender reads or recites a prepared statement of "I'm very sorry," and the church leaders then pressure the offended one, "Now it's your responsibility to forgive him." And the offended one, feeling more vulnerable and exposed than ever, just wanting to get the ordeal over with, says, "I forgive you." Is this the way forgiveness is really supposed to look?

Just as tears and words don't equal true repentance, true forgiveness can't necessarily be granted as easily as is it demanded. Though God stands with a posture of forgiveness for anyone in the world who will trust in Jesus Christ as his Savior, he doesn't actually forgive until that person does confess, repent, and trust in Jesus Christ.

In the Lord's Prayer, Jesus said, "Forgive us our debts as we forgive our debtors." Matthew 18:21–35 describes Peter asking the Lord if he should forgive an offending brother seven times. Jesus replied by telling the story of two debtors. Both of them recognized the reality of the great debt they owed. Both of them begged for an extended opportunity and vowed to make things right. Under these circumstances, Jesus admonishes all of us to forgive.

But if an offender never really acknowledges the enormity of his debt against the offended one, how is his debt to be truly released? What is an abuse survivor to do in those cases?

Crucial to the healing process is the *willingness* to have a forgiving heart and attitude. Hatred and seething anger will only deepen the pain and feeling of loss and isolation. This is a work that Jesus Christ alone can accomplish in the life of the believer, as He personally shows the one who was victimized His great love through His death on the cross, and His great power through His resurrection. Whether or not the offender ever seeks *true* forgiveness, the one who was victimized can be at peace.

WHAT FORGIVENESS IS NOT

The area I found to be the most difficult regarding Faith's dad and those who have excused his behavior is the relationship between forgiveness and holding the offender accountable. Three things have to be clear.

Forgiveness is not anyone else's prerogative

It's not at all uncommon to hear church members or university alumni or mission boards say, "Yes, he offended. But we've forgiven him." This is a great affront to the abuse survivor. If someone stole your life's savings, would it be appropriate for your pastor to say, "I've forgiven him for doing that"? No—forgiveness would be up to you.

Forgiveness is not forgetting

One abuse survivor said, "I was told to forgive and forget, so now I don't remember half my childhood." Is this really what our churches are demanding?

People who have been raped or molested may live with that nightmare the rest of their lives. Normal forgetting is usually not humanly possible.[135] Hopefully with God's love and a renewed focus on Him, some of the memories will lessen in intensity, but for church leaders to simply demand that victims of sexual abuse "forgive and forget" is neither reasonable nor biblical.

---

135   A different matter from "normal forgetting" is repression, in which people devastated by trauma have compartmentalized the abuse and blocked the memory of it from the rest of life. No caring Christian who understands this issue would wish repression on anyone. The concept of repression and retrieval of traumatic memories is an ongoing study that can be further explored in books such as Dr. Diane Langberg's *Counseling Survivors of Sexual Abuse* and websites such as www.globaltraumarecovery.org.

An abuse survivor may finally find the strength to come forward only to be told, "That was so long ago. You obviously didn't forgive, because you're still talking about it. You must be bitter." An abuse survivor wrote:

> I would be happy never to hear the word "bitterness" again. It seems that so many just paste that word to the forehead of everyone who has experienced abuse regardless of their response. It is just assumed that the victim MUST be bitter. It is the word that excuses the perpetrator. It is the word that condemns the victim, the word that makes them deserving of every bit of horror they endured.
>
> The victims are supposed to be quick to show instant forgiveness. Their hurt, confusion, pain are supposed to magically go away with the words "I forgive you" that they are supposed to quickly say. There is no time for them to grieve, for them to struggle, for them to have questions. They are not to question God. They are not to have nightmares or be confused in any way. To do so makes others uncomfortable. It is not neat and tidy. It doesn't seem like forgiveness, and aren't we all supposed to forgive?[136]

The facts are actually the opposite. In order to fully heal, abuse survivors need to understand what has happened to them and deal with it, and the only way this can be done is through their memories. When church leaders are quick to cut off the memory and record of the abuse, they bring great harm to the one who has been abused, which interferes with the healing process. Ministry leaders should never try to rob the abuse survivor of that need to fully deal with his

---

136   Personal correspondence, used by permission.

or her sexual abuse. Yes, even to refer back to it years later, perhaps as a connection point to the reason the survivor is struggling with something else.[137]

Forgiveness is not exemption from consequences

"The victim must realize that she [or he] can forgive without surrendering her [or his] desire for justice. . . .. God will be the judge, and he will mete out the punishments according to the crimes."[138]

Two entities have true authority to mete out judgment: God and government. God says in Romans 13:4 that the government is "God's minister, an avenger to execute wrath on him who practices evil." A well-regulated justice system will ideally make society safer not only by keeping the offender from the vulnerable so that he won't be able to commit further crimes against them, but also by striking fear into the hearts of those who would consider committing these crimes, when they see how sure and swift is the punishment.

But even if justice is never meted out on this earth, it is still coming. "'Vengeance is mine, I will repay,' says the Lord."[139] There will be a divine court date for all of those who have sexually abused the

---

137   These ideas are explored further in Chapters 10 and 12, "What Our Churches Must Do" and "How Family and Friends Must Help."

138   Victoria L. Johnson, *Restoring Broken Vessels: Confronting the Attack on Female Sexuality* (IVP Books, 2002), p. 88.

139   Romans 12:19. This Scripture may be used by some to silence victims of abuse, telling them that they should not seek justice or help because it is God's job to execute vengeance. But justice and vengeance are not the same thing. We can see how perverted this way of thinking is if we apply the same concept to a murder. If a man's beloved wife was murdered, would we tell him to just let it go because God will execute vengeance? No, for the safety and justice of our society, we report the crime so that the authorities can seek the murderer to bring him to justice. And we would believe it to be appropriate for the man who lost his wife to need to speak about the horror of his wife's murder, possibly again and again.

vulnerable and defenseless who have not truly repented with a willingness to bear the consequences.

In the Scriptures, there are some definite guidelines that need to be recognized. When God tells His people not to fellowship with someone who claims to be a Christian and who continues to habitually sin, is that unforgiving? When God tells us not even to eat with such a person, is that unforgiving? God told the Corinthian believers through the apostle Paul in 1 Corinthians 5:2 to "deliver such a one [a hard-hearted sinner] to Satan for the destruction of the flesh." Is that unforgiving? If so, then is God violating His own word?

Delivering this offender in the Corinthian church over to Satan for the destruction of his body was not being unforgiving. In the same way, for the government and even the church to hold a sexual offender accountable for his crime is not being unforgiving. And yet when some of us put God's Word into practice and hold offenders accountable for their sins and their lack of repentance, there are those in the church that will accuse us of being unforgiving. It is not unforgiving to obey the Word of God.

Those who surround sexual abuse survivors should protect them and seek justice, rather than telling them to be quiet, as Absalom did to Tamar, causing her to be desolate.[140] When abuse survivors see God's requirement for justice being pursued by their protectors, it becomes easier for them to be able to hold a stance of open-handed forgiveness for the personal debt that their offender will never be able to repay.

---

140   This story is told in 2 Samuel 13.

CHAPTER 9

BELIEVE AND SPEAK THE TRUTH ABOUT MERCY AND JUSTICE, GRACE AND LOVE

Mercy and justice, grace and love are all attributes of God that should be reflected in His people. But once again, they are commonly misunderstood. What are these qualities really, and what should they look like in our lives when we're dealing with offenders and victims?

HOW CAN WE SHOW MERCY?

Mercy is pity and compassion

Jesus said in Matthew 5:7, "Blessed are the merciful, for they shall obtain mercy." Our God is a God of mercy. He shows pity and compassion to the weak, downtrodden, and oppressed.

In the case of sexual abuse, it should be very clear that the oppressed is the one who was victimized. We have seen, though, that some people think when an alleged offender is accused of abuse that *he* is the one who is oppressed. This is an upside-down view of mercy.

By definition, perpetrators of sexual abuse have exercised power over their victims. Though not all abusers are men, the majority are, and especially in the context of churches and churchgoing families. One victim described the power differential this way:

> I learned that men were smart. They were intelligent. They were strong. They made the best decisions. We should follow them. . .. [T]hey had the power and the women were irrelevant. And my family structure is like that. My dad had all the power, and my mom had none.
>
> The church kind of taught us that men would be sexual, and they couldn't help it. But women shouldn't be. There were two kinds of women. The good kind and then the bad girls. But men had these sexual drives, and they couldn't help that. It's our job to control that.[141]

In exercising their abuse of power, offenders have shown no mercy to those they have violated. They have treated them with the opposite of mercy—with mercilessness, selfishness, malevolence, disdain, and the worst of cruelties.

Once the crime is revealed, enablers are often in place, ready to show their upside-down view of mercy—compassion for the abuser rather than the abused. In one court case of a young man who committed heinous sexual crimes against his sisters, other family members in their testimonies pleaded for mercy for him.[142] Is it compassion for the people of our churches to let a sexual predator go free in the name of mercy? Is it compassion to refrain from reporting

---

141   Annis, et al, *Set Us Free*, p. 18.

142   Jamie Dean, "The High Cost of Negligence," *World*, October 13, 2013, accessed via http://www.worldmag.com/2013/10/the_high_cost_of_negligence/page1.

him, but rather allow him to assault another innocent soul? When the victims become terrified and sickened by the calls for mercy for the offender, is it compassion for Christians to tell them to be silent? It seems that enablers are ready to brush aside the victims as if they are running over a stray cat, offering them no true mercy. Real mercy will show compassion to those who were hurt by the offenders and their crimes. Real compassion will try to prevent more sexual abuse by doing everything possible to see that offenders are behind bars where they can't prey on the vulnerable. This is true mercy.

Protecting the offender while silencing the victim is actually injustice under the guise of mercy.

Mercy comes when sins are confessed and forsaken

After his arrest and registration as a sex offender at the age of 72 and finally his excommunication, Faith's father began attending another church. The story of his child abuse came out in the papers (because I had called the papers and told them to run a story on it), so he had to go to the pastor of his new church.

"This problem I had with this girl, you know, pastor," he confided, "it was really her fault. She's one of these incorrigible teenagers, you know, one of those wild foster girls. Raging hormones. As for me, nothing like this has ever happened before. It was wrong, sure, but it's not who I am."

Somehow word got back to me that my father-in-law was attending fake counseling sessions. I called the pastor to make sure he knew the truth.

"Are you sure nothing like this has ever happened before?" the pastor asked him.

"Oh no, absolutely not. I'm just being persecuted—you know how it is when you're a Christian and a man of God."

"I have here before me," said the pastor, "a letter written by your daughter. She says that you confessed to raping her for nine years of her childhood."

"Where did you get that?" The child molester's face turned white, then red with anger.

"The DA already has a copy of everything I have here. You are no longer welcome at this church."

The sex offender's lawyer got permission for him to attend church in a different county, where the pastor was an old buddy of his. To the best of our knowledge, that's where he remains today.

Proverbs 28:13 says, "He who covers his sins will not prosper, but whoever *confesses* and *forsakes* them will have mercy." Here we see both *confession* and *repentance*, agreeing with God about the monstrous nature of one's sin and turning away from it to righteousness. When offenders are caught, they may try to dismiss their sin as if it's "just human nature," but there will be no mercy for those who stubbornly refuse to both confess and forsake their abuse of others. If there is no mercy from God, there should be no mercy from the church either, because we must walk God's way.

Jonah 2:8 says, "Those who regard worthless idols forsake their own mercy." It is the offender who forsakes mercy. It's not the fault of the victims or their supporters. When the offender made the decision to rape or molest one of God's children, he forsook his own mercy, and as long as he refuses to truly repent, he should expect none.

Mercy comes to those who fear God

Luke 1:50 says, "His mercy is on those who fear him." Does the person fear God who offends someone over whom he has gained control? One study found that child molesters average 49 victims and 114 acts of molestation.[143] How much fear of God do you think they have?

Can the offender find a place of mercy before God? Yes, but only when the fear of God has driven him to make a true confession of all his crimes against the victims and to forsake his evil ways. *Until then, he should live in terror every day because of what is awaiting him.*

Justice comes for those who do not fear God

In 1 John 1:9, we read, "If we confess our sins, He is faithful and just to forgive us our sins." Have you ever wondered why God uses the word *just* in this verse? How can a holy God be "just" in forgiving our sin? It is because when Jesus died on the cross, God the Father laid on his own Son the sins of all those who will make a true confession.

In Matthew 7:22–23 Jesus says, "Many will say to me in that day, 'Lord, Lord, have we not prophesied in your name, cast out demons in your name, and done many wonders in your name?' And then I will declare to them, 'I never knew you; depart from me, you who practice lawlessness!'" No doubt there will be many religious sexual offenders

---

143   Abel and Becker Child Molestation Prevention Study, 1983, cited in The Abel and Harlow Child Molestation Prevention Study, 2001, p. 10, which indicated that the earlier study may for several reasons have been more accurate. Accessed at http://www.cmrpi.org/pdfs/study.pdf.

in that group of people, expecting to hear God welcome them into heaven, only to hear Him say that He never knew them.

In Luke 16:24, Christ told about a rich man who died and went to hell. This man in his torment asked Abraham for water, but Abraham told him that was not possible. There is a place of mercy before God, but it must be sought in this life, and it must be sought with true confession and true repentance—or it will not be found. There is no mercy in hell.

Don't pervert justice

Proverbs 31:4–5 says, "It is not for kings to drink wine . . . lest they drink and forget the law, and pervert the justice of all the afflicted." *It is right to give justice for the sake of the afflicted.* Sadly, the justice needed by the afflicted ones is often being perverted in our churches as offenders who should be in jail are instead preaching in churches or serving as missionaries or being honored as someone who has been a great help to the ministry.

The truth is that justice must also stand alongside mercy or else you will have neither. Remember that mercy is compassion and pity—it is not the suspension of justice. If you want to show mercy to a sexual offender, pray for him and warn him of the peril he faces unless he confesses all of his sins and forsakes them. If you want to be merciful to a sexual offender, visit him in prison and speak to him of the justice and mercy of God.

Show mercy to the afflicted. Show justice to the ones who do the afflicting without repentance. God will do right. If we have His Holy Spirit in us, then His good works will flow out of us to do the same.

The abuse survivor who expressed frustration about the accusation of bitterness in chapter 8 also wrote the following:

> *I want to be angry at the sin of others, yet I need the same mercy they need. When I realize this, I pray for them. I do truly have compassion for them. I don't want them to face the eternal penalty of all they have done. I want them to taste the same mercy I have tasted. I pray that they will see God for who he is and be granted forgiveness, but I still hurt more for their victims.*[144]

HOW CAN WE SHOW GRACE?

"I tell you," a molesting pastor said to his elder board, "the only thing that kept me from going any farther with that teenage girl is the grace of God." We've heard some outrageous claims about God's grace.

Now to be sure, God's grace is truly amazing, and without it we would all be destined for hell. Ephesians 2:8–9 reminds us: "For by grace you have been saved through faith, and that not of yourselves; it is the gift of God, not of works, lest anyone should boast." God's grace is beautiful.

What God's grace doesn't do

Grace includes the outpouring of God's forgiveness to us when we come to Him in true confession and repentance. But does God's grace have boundaries? Can it really be used as a get-out-of-jail-free card? Is it a license to sin?

Consider what God says in Jude 1:4a: "For certain men have crept in unnoticed . . . who turned the grace of our God into lewdness."

---

144 Personal correspondence, used by permission.

The New International Version says they "pervert the grace of our God into a license for immorality." There are people who have crept into the church who are using God's grace as a cover to commit evil. They are trying to use it as a shortcut that bypasses true confession and true repentance. Sexual offenders and enablers want to point to the grace of God whenever the issues of sexual assault and domestic violence come up—almost as though "God's grace" is a magic wand that will make all of the accusations disappear and everyone go back to the placid façade. To them, grace is not an attribute of the holy God or the means by which God's plan for salvation and eternal life was given, or the power of transformation, but rather it is a convenient shield for their sin.

Sexual offenders also often think they are immune to God's anger because of His grace. In my first church, one man used to often tell me that I needed to preach "hell-fire-and-brimstone." Years later I was shocked to find out that he had raped all of his daughters. How could someone want me to preach "hell-fire-and-brimstone" when he was guilty of raping his daughters? The fact is that he thought he was exempt from judgment because of the grace of God. To him, God's grace was nothing more than a license to do whatever he wanted to do—which was to perpetrate great harm against his own children.

To use God's grace as a reason or excuse to sin is reprehensible. Romans 6:1–2 says, "Shall we continue in sin that grace may abound? Certainly not! How shall we who died to sin live any longer in it?" God's grace is beautiful, but when it is used as an excuse to sin and get away with it, the true meaning of God's grace is horribly distorted.

What God's grace does

In 1 Corinthians 15:10 the Apostle Paul said, "But by the grace of God I am what I am, and his grace toward me was not in vain; but I labored more abundantly than they all, yet not I, but the grace of God which was with me." The grace of God transformed Paul's life. Paul says that God's grace was at work in him to make him the person he came to be. Through the grace of God, Paul was empowered to live and walk in faith, to work with great zeal and energy for the kingdom and glory of God.

Sexual offenders count it very important to emphasize the forgiveness of God. They want to use God's grace as a type of force shield to protect their evil behavior, but in truth if the grace of God were at work in their lives at all, it would transform their lives toward godliness, not protect their sin.

So what is the truth about grace? God's grace does not protect our sinful condition. Instead, it radically transforms anyone who truly trusts in Christ, setting us on the right road, away from sin and toward righteousness.

In 2 Corinthians 9:8, God says, "God is able to make all grace abound toward you, that you, always having all sufficiency in all things, may have an abundance for every good work." The sexual offender or the enabler who so quickly claims the grace of God had better look again. Abusing a vulnerable soul is an evil work, not a good work, and has nothing to do with the grace of God. *God's grace produces good works, not evil ones.*

What will happen to those who scorn God's true grace?

Hebrews 10:29–31 contains a stern warning:

> Of how much worse punishment, do you suppose, will he
> be thought worthy who has trampled the Son of God un-
> derfoot, counted the blood of the covenant by which he
> was sanctified a common thing, and insulted the Spirit of
> grace? For we know him who said, "Vengeance is Mine, I
> will repay," says the Lord. And again, "The LORD will judge
> his people." *It is a fearful thing to fall into the hands of the liv-
> ing God.* (Italics added.)

I think of my father-in-law with his arrogance and cockiness, claiming the grace of God and the blood of Christ, raping and molesting his daughter from the time she was nine until she was almost 18. While he pastored different churches, he served and took communion with no regard for his sin, never confessing this crime to God, never asking Faith for forgiveness. All those years, until he was found out at the age of 72, he had been trampling underfoot the Son of God and insulting the Spirit of grace. In our last conversation, when we finally cut off our relationship with him, he was completely unashamed of himself and what he had done.

The words of Hebrews 10:29–31 are absolutely terrifying. For sexual offenders who claim to be Christians and yet so disregard God's Word and force their control and lust on precious vulnerable souls, they should read this passage and fear God. They should be on their faces before God and their victims, begging for forgiveness. How can a man who spent most of his life raping and molesting children possibly think that God's grace and favor is toward him? This is delusional indeed.

Hebrews makes it clear that it is the Spirit of God's grace that these devious wrongdoers are insulting. But no matter how he twists, manipulates, and distorts the grace of God, the offender will never be able to cover his sin. God is not interested in covering or hiding sin—he wants to forgive it and bring restoration. That happens only when individuals truly confess, completely repent, and put their faith and trust in Jesus Christ, through the finished work of His sacrificial death and victorious resurrection and ascension.

How do we as the people of God show grace to offenders?

The best way to show grace to an offender is to call him to truth and righteousness, humility and repentance, by which, through the power of God, his life can be truly transformed.

So how do I show grace for my father-in-law, when he raped and molested my wife for much of her childhood? We have called him to repentance. We have brought him to accountability. These are the most gracious acts we can do for an unrepentant offender. Because we have chosen to obey God's Word and are now seeking to hold him accountable for his sin when he refuses to acknowledge wrongdoing, we have no contact with him.

When I look at the evidence in my father-in-law's life, I see nothing that points to God's presence. But I truly don't want him to spend eternity in hell. I pray that someday before it's eternally too late, he'll know what it means to be truly repentant. My hope is that one day we'll walk together in heaven, with all of our sins behind us, with not so much as a thought of sin, redeemed and transformed children of God. This will be the end result of grace.

God wants to extend His grace to all. The author of Hebrews—the same author who gave the dire warning about grace—encouraged his reader to come boldly to God. In 4:16 we read, "Let us therefore come boldly to the *throne of grace,* that we may obtain mercy and *find grace* to help in time of need."

The sexual offender as well as anyone else can come humbly in true confession and true repentance, and yet confidently because of the sacrifice of Jesus Christ. There he can seek God's forgiveness and transforming, powerful grace.

HOW CAN WE SHOW LOVE?

Speaking Truth in Love

The theme verse for our ministry is Ephesians 4:15: "But, speaking the truth in love, [you] may grow up in all things into Him who is the head—Christ."

When victims report the sexual offender to the law, or even if they go to their church leaders to try to find help, they often hear that they are not being loving.

> *"Why does she keep talking about that?" After the wall of silence came down, the seemingly inevitable undercurrent of unrest seethed in our church. "How can they say those things about her father?"*

> *"Why can't they just let the past be the past?"*

> *"How can they be so unloving?"*

We have some questions too.

Why would any Christian tell people who are trying to stop sexual abuse that they are being unloving? Are some Christians so blind to the most basic truths of Scripture?

Are they caring only for the offender? Are they overlooking the vulnerable ones he was raping and molesting?

Proverbs 18:5 says, "It is not good to be partial to the wicked or to deprive the innocent of justice" (NIV). If we hide the sin, we are being partial to the wicked. If we protect the offender, we are being partial to the wicked. If we ask victims not to tell anyone, we deprive the innocent of justice. When we fail to report offenders, we deprive the innocent of justice.

Who is really being unloving?

Romans 12:9 states, "Love must be sincere. Hate what is evil; cling to what is good." True love, God's love, will never embrace evil. When the sexual offender harms his victim, he is not being loving, but evil. When the offender lies about what he has done, he is not being loving, but evil. When the enablers spread the lies of the offender, they are not being loving, but evil. When the enablers attack the victim with their words, they are not being loving, but evil.

Do these seem like harsh statements?

Jesus also used harsh words in Matthew 16:23 when Peter said that death on a cross would never happen to his Lord. "Get behind me, Satan!" Jesus replied. "You are an offense to me, for you are not mindful of the things of God but the things of men." In a similar way, when enablers try to silence abuse survivors and ridicule them and call them "unloving" and "unforgiving," they are doing the work of Satan.

First Corinthians 13:5 reminds us that love "does not seek its own." When someone begins raping and molesting, what he is doing is "seeking his own." He is selfish and thus becomes incapable of true love. To lead a selfish life is to live a life without love.

And why do enablers protect the sexual offender and reject the one who was victimized? They, too, are selfish and unloving. They are worried about themselves, they don't want to be embarrassed, and they are concerned about how this situation will affect them or their ministry. If love and selfishness cannot coexist, then the enablers are also refusing to love as long as they are enabling. Paul's words in Romans 13:10 are clear: "Love does no harm to a neighbor." The offenders and their enablers have done and are still doing terrible harm to their victims.

In contrast, God is raising up some courageous souls to confront this evil, who are enduring ridicule and rejection in order to protect God's precious ones. Now *that* is true love in action.

The consequences of failing to show love for the oppressed and vulnerable

Be sure of this, unless they change, the offenders and the enablers will pay a heavy price for their deeds. They are the ones being unloving, and they would do well to remember Jesus' warning in Matthew 18:10: "Take heed that you do not despise one of these little ones, for I say to you that in heaven their angels always see the face of my Father who is in heaven." Anyone who is even thinking about harming a little one had better think twice, because those children have angels standing in the presence of God on their behalf, and anyone who despises one of these little ones will pay a price.

When enablers surround the offender, attempting to conceal his sin and relocate him to another ministry that will ultimately allow him to rape and molest again, these blind leaders of the blind will, as Jesus said, lead many to destruction. I tell you, the blood and tears of those precious souls who have been violated will be on their hands, and God will deal with them accordingly.

God is not a liar. Will He ignore His own warnings?

What does real love look like?

When the victim has the courage to stand up and tell his or her story in order to protect others who are vulnerable, that is love. When anyone finds the courage to tell the truth about this evil and confronts an offender or an enabler and thereby protect others, that is love. When individuals begin to value the weak and oppressed at least as much as the powerful and controlling, that is love.

It is far from unloving to encourage abuse survivors to tell their stories. Listening to them in love without any shame or blame can be an important part of their healing process. Times of mourning and lamenting in our churches can be a call for the people of the church to "not harden their hearts," as God warns His people in Hebrews 3, but instead to remain tender and sensitive to the voice of God in their lives. This can lead to repentance, not just for the offenders, but for the enablers and the ignorant.

It is not unloving for us to encourage victims to hope for and expect justice. It is not unloving to expect the church to obey the Word of God and to confront the sexual offender and to hold him accountable. It is not unloving to expect the church to set strict boundaries around a sexual offender in order to protect other children. It is not unloving for a church to shun a sexual offender who has not brought forth fruits worthy of repentance.

Protecting the weakest and most vulnerable among us is one of the most loving things we can do.

When we love rightly, we will love the Truth

First Corinthians 13:6 says that love "does not rejoice in iniquity, but rejoices in the truth." It's one or the other. As long as church leaders refuse to embrace the truth about this issue and what God's Word says we must do about it, they too are being unloving. Second Thessalonians 2:9–10 says,

> The coming of the lawless one is according to the working of Satan, with all power, signs, and lying wonders, and with all unrighteous deception among those who perish, *because they did not receive the love of the truth,* that they might be saved. (Italics added.)

This Scripture warns that people will embrace deception and reject the love of the truth. The truth is that by the time they are eighteen years old, one out of three girls and one out of every six boys will be raped or molested.[145] This is a tragic and evil epidemic. The truth is that in regard to this issue, there is little difference between the church community and the non-church community. The tragic

---

145   J. Briere, and D. M. Eliot, "Prevalence and Psychological Sequence of Self-Reported Childhood Physical and Sexual Abuse in General Population." *Child Abuse & Neglect,* 2003, Vol. 27, Issue 10, pp. 1205–1222.

evil is in our midst. The truth is that when it comes to sexual abuse, *the people in our churches have embraced deception.*

When Christians turn from this deception and embrace the truth, when we weep, mourn, and pray for God's forgiveness and for His help and power to change the tragic condition of our churches . . . that is love. When we humble ourselves and cry out to God about this sin in our midst, then I believe that God will respond to our pleas.

To reject the truth is to live in deception and ultimately to reject love. Jesus spoke in Matthew 25 about caring for "the least of these," indicating the importance of showing love to ones who are not powerful and influential. If we as the church fail to protect these most vulnerable souls in our midst, than how can we be credible in anything we do?

PART THREE

TAKE
RESPONSIBILITY
AND ACTION

CHAPTER 10

WHAT OUR CHURCHES MUST DO

In terms of dealing with sexual abuse in the church, the first thing you have to do is give people permission to speak about it. I know of actually a pastor and his wife who are on the road of recovery from sexual abuse. And not a single person in the congregation knows about it, because they are afraid that, if they share that with anyone, they're going to be ousted from the church and rejected. So the church has to get to a point were [sic] it can accept dealing with sexual abuse. [146]

That quotation above isn't about Faith and me, but it well could have been. For over twenty years we walked the road of recovery alone and silent, just assuming—without even a fully formed thought— that we shouldn't talk about it.

God has set before us a clear path in his Word that gives us principles and guidelines for dealing with virtually any situation. In order to fully deal with abuse, everyone's thinking needs to change

---

146 Annis, et al, *Set Us Free*, p. 97.

according to the Word of God, and our churches must lead the way in getting it right. Christian churches have for too long muddled their way through this issue and for the most part have dealt with it according to the wisdom of man and not the wisdom of God. For the most part, abusers and their enablers have ruled the day.

CONFESS AND REPENT OF OUR FAILURE TO DEAL WITH THIS SIN BIBLICALLY

Woe to those who *decree unrighteous decrees,* who write misfortune, which they have prescribed *to rob the needy of justice,* and to take what is right from the poor of my people, that widows may be their prey, and that they may rob the fatherless. What will you do in the day of punishment, and in the desolation which will come from afar? To whom will you flee for help? And where will you leave your glory? Without me they shall bow down among the prisoners, and they shall fall among the slain. For all this his anger is not turned away, but his hand is stretched out still.[147] (Italics added.)

No more policies and procedures to avoid helping the abused

God is outraged by those who "make decrees" in order to rob the needy of justice. When I read about these unrighteous decrees, I think of the ministry leaders who have written policies and procedures to silence the voices of the violated ones and their families. God is outraged![148]

---

147 Isaiah 10:1–4.

148 Perhaps more than any other "decree," the no-gossip policy has served to keep abused people silent about their abuse, with the ostensible purpose of preventing anyone from "speaking evil" of anyone else. In the CD sermon "Gossip: The Plague of the Church" (Vision Forum, 2007), Scott Brown, director of the Na-

God admonished Israel over and over in the book of Jeremiah to repent, but they would not, and they paid a heavy price. Right up until the end, the false prophets were sure that God's blessing would soon be restored, and they tried to silence any voice like Jeremiah's who called for repentance. Many churches are doing the same things today. Judgment is near, and we continue playing church as though there were nothing wrong.

If you've been sexually assaulted and feel as if God doesn't care and somehow overlooks what this evil person has done to you, please read and hear what God is saying to offenders and enablers in these verses. "They shall fall among the slain," and even that will not appease His anger over what the policymakers have done to deprive you of justice.

No more saying "That's not my problem"

Speaking specifically of the unspeakable crime of clergy sexual abuse, psychologist Dr. Diane Langberg says,

> As long as we continue to define leadership as the world does—a position demanding expertise and charisma— we will breed leaders who . . . will be broken off from a

tional Center for Family-Integrated Churches, described a conversation with a pastor friend. He said that this pastor told new members, "No one will speak evil of you behind your back." Brown then went on to say about himself, "I thought what a great policy and what a great practice in the church. . . ." In another sermon from the same organization, in the context of explaining how speaking the truth can be a step toward divorce, another preacher said, "There is a time when telling the truth is not a blessing; it is a curse." (Dan Horn, "The Tongue Is Fire," sermon available at www.ncfic.org.) Though the no-gossip rule is presented as a policy to prevent anyone in the church from speaking evil of others, we have seen that in practice it is about keeping the oppressed from "speaking evil" of their oppressors. When someone in a position of power or perceived power is actually *committing* evil, the one on whom the evil is perpetrated cannot speak out for fear of "gossip" and has nowhere to turn.

reciprocal relationship with the body they are called to serve. Once reciprocity has broken down, then good is defined not as what is good for the body, but rather what is good for the isolated self. This climate is a perfect set-up for the abuse of others. . . . The problem of clergy sexual abuse is not simply about [sexual abuse. It is also] . . . about a church whose members have abdicated their responsibilities.[149]

In *This Little Light: Beyond a Baptist Preacher Predator and His Gang*, Christa Brown details the stonewalling of leaders in the Southern Baptist Convention to deal with predators in their midst, citing "church autonomy" as the reason.[150] In essence, each person in each church is given an excuse to turn a blind eye to evil in any other Southern Baptist church. Joe Trull, an ethics expert with the Southern Baptist Convention, acknowledged the problem:

> Decentralized denominations such as the Southern Baptist Convention and many evangelical bodies have no national policies, leaving each individual church to establish its own guidelines. Sexual misconduct is routinely covered up in these settings. Dee Ann Miller, a victims' advocate and author of books on the topic, has recorded complaints from

---

149   Diane Langberg, Ph.D., "Clergy Sexual Abuse," in C.C. Kroeger and J.R. Beck, eds, *Abuse, Women, and the Bible* (Grand Rapids: Baker Books, 1996), pp. 63, 68, accessed via http://www.dianelangberg.com/work/articles/ClergySexualAbuse.pdf. Dr. Langberg takes pains in this article and elsewhere to explain that "members" means more than those who have signed a statement of membership. "Members" are parts of the body, who ache together when there is pain anywhere in the body, according to 2 Corinthians 12.

150   Brown, *This Little Light*, pp. 91, 138, 142–143, 155, 168.

victims in thirty states, half of them involving minors. Church officials largely have not been responsive.[151]

The more closed and isolated the church or group—even from each other—the more opportunities there are for abuse. Because of the claim of "church autonomy," some victim advocates are calling for a restructuring of church hierarchies. We need to do everything we can to put safeguards in place in order to protect our children, but until change takes place at the heart level, all the policies in world will not be enough to keep children safe. When leaders are corrupt and driven by selfish desires, they will find a way around the rules.

People who love God within our churches need to expose offenders, even if the offenders move to other churches. They need to share that information publicly without fear of being accused of "gossip," so that the weakest among us can be protected. No matter what the hierarchical structure of a church or denomination, we must all see the need to care for the "least of these." We must all say, "Yes, this is our problem. We will help."

Proverbs 29:27 says, "An unjust man is an abomination to the righteous, and he who is upright in the way is an abomination to the wicked." With so many church leaders acting as enablers for sexual abuse offenders, we are left with no choice but to conclude that many of our church leaders are in fact wicked themselves. To protect that which is evil, is in fact to be evil.

True confession: Agree with God that our refusal to acknowledge this sin is an affront to Him.

---

151   Joe E. Trull and James E. Carter, *Ministerial Ethics: Moral Formation for Church Leaders* (Grand Rapids: Baker Academic, 2004), p. 162.

True repentance: Turn from ignoring and covering sexual abuse, and go in the right direction.

This is a description of myself. As my eyes opened more and more in 2005 and 2006, I made a true confession before God that I had been blindly ignoring this abomination. I turned from my wrongdoing of ignoring and implicitly covering it, and I began going in a different direction. The right one.

Awake, you who sleep, arise from the dead, and Christ will give you light.[152]

ADDRESS SEXUAL ASSAULT AS A CRIME

Educate the people of God

> *The pastor, several of the church leaders, and various members in the church knew my sisters and I were being molested by my father. But no one in the church said or did anything. I heard plenty of sermons and Bible lessons teaching that girls should not have sex before marriage. But I'd never heard anybody preach a sermon or give a warning to fathers not to have sex with their daughters.*[153]

In *When Child Abuse Comes to Church,* Bill Anderson urges us that "education is the first line of defense in protecting our children."[154] Before a church can truly prepare itself to deal with sexual abuse, it needs to educate, through books like this one and other resources.[155] If youth groups can talk about the importance of refraining from sex before marriage, then they can talk about what sexual abuse is

---

152   Ephesians 5:14.

153   Johnson, *Restoring Broken Vessels*, p. 95.

154   Anderson, *When Child Abuse Comes to Church*, p. 11.

155   The Bibliography and the Resources Appendix offer many helpful resources that can be used to help educate the people of a church about sexual abuse.

and why it's a crime, clearly explaining that the victim is not at fault and needs to find someone safe to tell. If we had been taught what to do, Faith and I would have handled the aftermath of her sexual abuse much differently. But through our growing-up years in Christian environments, we never once heard anyone speak about sexual abuse, not once. We were totally unprepared to deal with what her father had done to her.

Those who are charged to lead God's people are perpetuating a culture of ignorance from one generation of Christians to the next. With the wall of silence in place, is it any wonder that people in our churches have no clue what to do when abuse comes to light?

At a conference I heard a well-known speaker share with brokenness about his father's moral failure. I took the opportunity to talk with him about the need to speak out from church pulpits about sexual abuse. But he resisted the idea, saying that if pastors simply preached about righteousness and sin in general that this somehow was going to cover the issue. Our Christian leaders speak openly about controversial and "private" moral issues such as sex before marriage, homosexuality, and abortion. But for some reason, sexual abuse still hides behind the Wall of Silence. This is the mindset that has gotten our churches in the crisis situation we're in today.

In John 8:32, Christ says, "You shall know the truth, and the truth shall make you free." Only by speaking the truth about the great violation that is sexual assault, all its ramifications and the harm it causes, can our churches be free to offer the great hope that is found in Jesus Christ. Lack of knowledge enslaves a people, but the truth sets them free.

Take responsibility for those who are more vulnerable

Although anyone who hears firsthand of a crime can report it to the police, mandatory reporters (clergy, counselors, etc.)[156] who hear firsthand of a case of child sexual abuse can be liable for committing a criminal offense if they do not report it to the police—they don't need to verify it first, and they may do damage to the situation if they try to.

The woman who was raped and molested throughout her sixth-grade year by her teacher in her Christian school wrote:

> *One time when I locked myself in the bathroom at school, he beat on the door so hard that the frame began to crack. Another teacher came by and asked him what was going on. He convinced her I was being bad and had locked myself in the bathroom, and she walked away. To me that was just one more proof that what he told me was true. No one would believe me, and I would be sent back to his classroom again.[157]*

We cannot afford to close our eyes to "the appearance of evil"[158] that is being perpetrated right under our noses. We all must always be aware. The most clever offenders will not stand out as horrible,

---

156   The definition of "mandatory reporter" varies by state. If you have any position in a church, even a volunteer position, you must be aware of your state's definition of mandatory reporter.

157   Personal correspondence, used by permission.

158   1 Thessalonians 5:22, KJV.

depraved men. They'll very often be the last ones you would suspect. That is, unless you keep your eyes and ears open and don't just walk away.

Take measures to make our churches a safe place to report abuse

Our churches must make it very clear, from the pulpits, in Sunday school, in children's church, in youth groups, in small group Bible studies, in women's meetings and men's meetings, that we want abuse victims to report their abuse and not keep it secret (even if the statute of limitations is long past, as is often the case in cases of sexual abuse). Christa Brown made her recommendations for Southern Baptists, but every denomination, every family of churches, every association, every networked group of churches and ministries, every independent body would do well to do the same:[159]

1. Provide "a safe and welcoming place" where abuse survivors, especially those whose cases cannot be criminally prosecuted (for example, because the statute of limitations is past), can report clergy sex abuse.

2. Provide an "objective, trained panel" for responsibly assessing abuse reports in cases that cannot be reported to the police.[160]

3. Provide a database of profiled clergy sex offenders who would not be found on a background check of those who have been criminally prosecuted, for example, those who have confessed to the crime or those in whose cases there is irrefutable evidence.[161]

---

159   Christa Brown, www.stopbaptistpredators.org.

160   The organization Godly Response to Abuse in the Christian Environment (GRACE) is an example of a highly-qualified team of independent professionals who could responsibly assess abuse reports when police reports are not an option. See www.netgrace.org.

161   Christa Brown's plea was made in 2009. In 2015, though the SBC has helped to facilitate criminal background checks for its member churches, to date there

No matter who it is that reports the alleged abuse, no matter who the allegation is against, the accusation must be taken seriously.

Allow the legal authorities to do their job

At a workshop that presented a case study in which a deacon molested a boy, some people insisted that before going to the police, the pastor should first "determine" whether or not the story was true or credible. This may seem reasonable, but the fact is that it's *not* the pastor's job to determine credibility. Pastors don't have the skills or the legal authority to conduct an investigation. These efforts, which might be well-meaning, can end up allowing the offender a chance to hide evidence and threaten anyone who may have knowledge of the particular incident, further endangering the victims. It is the criminal investigator's job, not ours, to determine if an accusation is credible. Church leaders and members should realize that any steps they take on their own may be obstructing justice.

If a child is making an allegation, the people of God have a moral and biblical, and in many cases even legal, obligation to report offenders to authorities. In the case of one who was over the age of consent when he or she was assaulted, the church should make sure the victim knows that he or she can report to the police when ready, and will be supported no matter which decision is made.[162]

Legal authorities such as the police force, investigators, and the department of social services are trained to conduct a proper

---

is still no informational database available to SBC churches of clergy sex offenders who have never been criminally prosecuted but have admitted their crimes or have irrefutable evidence against them.

162   The age of consent and other legal and technical matters pertaining to sexual assault vary by state. It is crucial that each church body understand the laws in their own state. Ignorance breeds more abuse.

investigation, have the legal authority to take evidence, and can even take a child out of a dangerous situation.[163] The system isn't perfect and will make mistakes, but God has put government in place to punish those who do evil. This may be agonizing for some, if the child is being taken out of the home, but the most important thing is for the child to be safe. That is all the more reason for the church to stop being a sanctuary for offenders and to start being known as a place of safety for those who have been sexually abused.[164]

Actively seek to prevent abuse

The church needs to make sure that there are preventative measures in place to help stop abuse in the church context before it starts. Action items such as background checks on children's workers, windows in classroom doors, policies that require more than one adult with children at all times, and making sure that churches have training each year for their church staff are some of the minimum requirements that need to be attended to in local churches.[165]

Many church leaders seem to want to make a quick statement that condemns this evil—because no one would openly say they support it!—and then move on to other things. But the task that the church is facing demands diligence and a daily effort until Christ

---

163   Ideally churches could have foster families ready to receive children who need to be removed from their homes.

164   Bill Anderson's book *When Child Abuse Comes to Church* provides an instructive picture of the various aspects involved in unraveling a complicated case of sexual abuse in a church context.

165   To institute robust policies for protecting their children, church leaders will benefit from reading Voyle Glover's *Protecting Your Church Against Sexual Predators: Legal FAQs for Church Leaders* (Grand Rapids: Kregel Academic & Professional, 2005), and Deepak Reju's *On Guard: Preventing and Responding to Child Abuse* (Greensboro: New Growth Press, 2014).

returns for His children. This battle, like all battles, must be fought with vigilance in order to be won. It is time for Christians to come together to engage this fight to protect the children and other vulnerable people that God has placed in our care.

> *I would like to see a church be honest enough to admit that sexual abuse has and is taking place in their congregation. Brave enough to address it openly, making it difficult and uncomfortable for abusers to feel safe. Caring enough to commit themselves to walking with victims of sexual abuse. Wise enough to set guidelines in place for the protection of God's precious little children that he entrusted to their care. Discerning enough to know how to handle accusations, and diligent enough to hold abusers accountable.*[166]

HELP THOSE WHO HAVE BEEN AFFECTED BY THE ABUSE

Once the church has turned over the alleged perpetrator to the law, we must focus on our God-given responsibility of ministering to the needs of those who have been harmed and deeply affected by the abuse. Church leaders must give the victim or victims and their families first priority.

Don't miss the fact that the offender's family may also be reeling from this accusation. The offender's spouse and children may have been taken by surprise by the offender's actions and may be devastated. They shouldn't be shunned or ignored, but should receive offers of love as well.[167]

---

166   Annis, et al, *Set Us Free,* pp. 188–119.

167   Though we have heard many stories of enabling family members who turned a blind eye to the most appalling abuse, there are also cases in which the family members were completely stunned by the revelation that there was

When both the victim and the sexual offender attend the same church, the ramifications affect most, if not all, of the people. Church members are hurting, embarrassed, and angry. There are many questions about what will happen and how it will affect them and their church.

Have a counseling plan already in place

When a house is on fire, that's no time to begin to make the plan for how to deal with fire. Churches need to have a plan in place for dealing with any incidences of sexual assault long before any occurs, establishing relationships with reputable Christian counselors and professionally trained trauma counselors.[168] It would be ideal to offer financial assistance for this counseling, not simply to avoid legal liability, but because this is the loving thing to do.[169]

At one church where we spoke, the pastor already had a plan in place to deal with sexual abuse. Godly and knowledgeable Christian women who had gone through sexual abuse or were familiar with the issue were ready to walk the journey of healing with those who

---

a sexual offender in their midst. For example, in 2012 Donald Ratcliff, a well-respected professor at Wheaton College, pleaded guilty to possession of aggravated child pornography (under age thirteen). Only a few months later his wife (and later ex-wife) Brenda began chronicling her journey of despair and hope in discovering that she was the wife of a pedophile. She blogs at "A Solitary Journey," www.brendafindingelysium.blogspot.com.

168   A woman who is raw and vulnerable from sexual abuse should be cautioned to avoid solitary counseling with a male counselor. The stories are many in which women who have been violated seek counseling but are then sexually assaulted by their male counselors. There is a reason for the guideline found in Titus 2:3–5 that the older women should teach the younger ones about the complex issues of life and godliness. If counseling does take place with a man, appropriate measures should be in place to help the woman feel safe at all times. For example, she should feel free to record the counseling session.

169   The Resources Appendix gives ideas for ways to find further help.

had experienced the trauma of sexual assault. These ladies would help guide wounded women through the process of sharing their stories and getting counseling and any other help that was needed.

Some churches, in reviewing their counseling plan, may find that, as chapter 5 described, they have been abuse enablers—and even re-abusers—through what they thought was good biblical counseling. Often this destructive counseling happened not with evil intent but simply through ignorance. If this has been the case, then openness to listening to past mistakes would be appropriate, with heartfelt confession and true repentance, finding the people they hurt if at all possible and asking for forgiveness, seeking to encourage the abuse survivor with hope in Jesus Christ through the healing journey.[170]

Consider support groups

Leading or helping to lead a support group for people who have gone through abuse can help in the healing process. Some of the best leaders and facilitators are those who have survived abuse and have gone through support groups themselves. Faith has led a support group with the book *Surviving the Secret*.[171] A single mom who had endured domestic abuse took a Living Waters course, and afterwards, a changed woman, she started working with others in a Living Waters group.[172] She later led her future husband to the Lord, and now they are doing Living Waters courses together in the Netherlands. Other materials can also offer help.[173] Sometimes the

---

170   See Chapter 13, "The Abuse Survivor's Shepherd."

171   Rodriguez and Vredevelt, *Surviving the Secret*.

172   Desert Stream/Living Waters Ministries can be viewed at www.desert-stream.org.

173   Several possible helps for group study are listed in the Resources Appendix.

best help for the abuse survivor is simply in finding out that he or she is not alone.

Be willing to walk the long journey of healing

In 1 Thessalonians 2:7–11 Paul says, "But we were gentle among you, just as a nursing mother cherishes her own children . . . you know how we exhorted, and comforted, and charged every one of you, as a father does his own children." Paul describes his relationship with the people at the church in Thessalonica as being like that of the caring mother and a devoted father, gently helping and nurturing.

The Bible exhorts those who love Christ to support the weak and oppressed. Christians need to understand that healing from sexual assault may take many years.

> *Maybe the church needs to teach people just how to listen and how to not panic when someone falls apart in their presence. I mean the real struggle is, if someone would talk to me about what I was experiencing during the church service, someone who observed that I was falling apart, their first reaction might be panic and maybe the message that the church needs to send is, teach the people not to panic. Teach the people that we are all strugglers on the way and that what's important is that you recognize that and you just be willing to listen to someone else's struggle and not try to fix it.*[174]

Weep with those who weep

Our churches must not fear lamentation. The psalmist David didn't shy away from it. The prophet Jeremiah actively engaged in it.

---

174   Annis, et al, *Set Us Free*, p. 98.

Asaph, Daniel, Ezra, Nehemiah, and many more people in the Bible all knew how to mourn.

We live on the other side of the death and resurrection of Jesus. We of all people have reason to rejoice in the strong foundation of His victory. And yet . . .

We still live on this side of eternity. Sin and evil are still among us. Instead of viewing lament as a lack of faith, we would do well to view it as part of the process of faith.

Lament requires humility. It also requires a deeper level of faith than the constant happy-happy that is preached from many pulpits. It takes a deeper level of faith to cry out to God with our voices, "Things are not right. We see that. We are looking to you to make them right."

> It is crucial to comprehend a lament is as far from complaining or grumbling as a search is from aimless wandering. A grumbler has already reached a conclusion, shut down all desire, and postures with questions that are barely concealed accusations. . . . But a lament involves even deeper emotion because a lament is truly asking, seeking, and knocking to comprehend the heart of God.[175]

Though we know that in Christ we are ultimately victorious, the earthly consequences of evil still give reason to mourn. There is even reason to mourn and grieve collectively, as a church body. One abuse survivor wrote:

---

175   Dan Allender, "The Hidden Hope in Lament," *Mars Hill Review,* premier issue, 1994, pp. 25-38, accessed via http://www.leaderu.com/marshill/mhr01/lament1.html.

For expressing grief and anger, it really helps that my church sings the Psalms. When we first visited, it was the Psalms that began to thaw me out, make me feel again and hear again what was going on in church. It was about a year and a half of serious triggers, PTSD, and a few deeply suicidal weeks before things leveled out to the place where I thought I might be able to lament without being swallowed up in despair. The Psalms are short enough that in singing or praying through them you don't get stuck in the place you actually are. It as though you are given a chance to practice coming out on the other side of your anger against God and end with praise or at least acceptance.[176]

We all need that chance to practice coming out on the other side of our anger against God, ending with praise, or at least acceptance.

> The lament psalms, then, are a complaint that makes the shrill insistence that: (1) Things are not right in the present arrangement. (2) They need not stay this way and can be changed. (3) The speaker will not accept them in this way, for the present arrangement is intolerable. (4) It is God's obligation to change things.[177]

Our churches can weep with those who weep by, among other things, participating together in a Service of Lament for those whose innocence was exploited, whose trust was broken, whose spirit was crushed.[178] Yes, we have confidence that our victorious Lord Jesus is

---

176   Personal correspondence, used by permission.

177   Walter Brueggemann, "The Costly Loss of Lament," *The Psalms: The Life of Faith*, edited by Patrick D. Miller. (Minneapolis: Fortress, 1995, pp. 98-111. Originally published by the author in *JSOT* 36 (1986) 57-71.

178   Chapter 14 shows in memoir form a sample Service of Lament. More information about conducting your own Service of Lament can be found on the

the ultimate Healer, and biblical lament will always end with hope in him. But it is appropriate for us to mourn the temporal consequences of the evil.

> People like Job, David, Jeremiah, and even Jesus reveal to us that prayers of complaint can still be prayers of faith. They represent the last refusal to let go of the God who may seem to be absent or worse—uncaring. If this is true, then lament expresses one of the most intimate moments of faith—not a denial of it. It is supreme honesty before a God whom my faith tells me I can trust. He encourages me to bring everything as an act of worship, my disappointment, frustration, and even my hate. Only lament uncovers this kind of new faith, a biblical faith that better understands God's heart as it is revealed through Jesus Christ.[179]

UNDERSTAND OUR RESPONSIBILITY TO THE OFFENDER

If he is truly repentant

Most sexual offenders have developed the skills of lying, deceiving, and manipulating to the extent that the average person is easily deceived, and this includes even counselors and ministry leaders. A truly repentant sexual offender will make his repentance obvious through his willingness to follow through with the consequences of

---

Speaking Truth in Love website, www.speakingtruthinlove.org.

179   Michael Card, *A Sacred Sorrow: Reaching Out to God in the Lost Language of Lament* (Colorado Springs: NavPress, 2005), pp. 30-31.

his sin, bringing forth fruits of repentance.[180] After he has served his legal sentence, a specialized, long-term rehabilitation program that provides counseling with someone familiar with the devious ways of sexual offenders would be ideal. Our churches need to develop more residential facilities that are designed to help repentant offenders to find rehabilitation and restoration.[181]

If, according to his counsel, the offender cannot attend church, then finding an off-site location where he can worship would be best. He may need to get his teaching and fellowship from a small group gathering where he can worship and learn and pray with other Christians without being a danger to children.

If a repentant offender can legally and safely attend church (according to the licensed, professionally trained sex-offender counseling he is receiving), that church needs to make sure to set and enforce proper boundaries, mandating that a responsible mentor will be with him and monitoring him at all times, including in the parking lot and in the bathrooms. These boundaries and limitations will need to be in place for the rest of his life. The church must ensure the safety of the children at all times, and if they can't do that, then the offender shouldn't attend. Though it may sound harsh, these boundaries are really a way that the church is showing love and care for the offender, to protect him from sin as well as protecting children from him.

If he is not repentant

Matthew 18 gives guidance for following through with church discipline. Though this guidance is regarding personal offenses and

---

180   This topic is addressed further in Chapter 11, "What the Offender Must Do."
181   See the Resources Appendix.

not criminal offenses, which need to be reported to the police, it still provides practical steps for dealing with recalcitrant church members. This guideline would be assuming that the case is making its way through the legal system or else that the case cannot be tried. After the one who has sinned has been approached by an individual (never the victim, but a leader in the church), and then with two or three, the Scripture says, "And if he refuses to hear them, tell it to the church. But if he refuses even to hear the church, let him be to you like a heathen and a tax collector." If an offender is not repentant, the church needs to be prepared to exercise church discipline against him, which will mean severing all ties except to admonish the unrepentant one to turn to Christ. Only when an offender has given up all of his defenses can there be any progress in bringing about meaningful change in his life.

Proverbs 28:4 reminds us, "Those who forsake the law praise the wicked, but such as keep the law contend with them." If we love God's Word, we will take a stand against unrepentant sexual offenders in the church.

HUMBLE OURSELVES AND PRAY

Ezra 10:1–2 says, "Now while Ezra was praying, and while he was confessing, weeping, and bowing down before the house of God, a very large assembly of men, women, and children gathered to him from Israel; for the people wept very bitterly . . . 'We have trespassed against our God.'"

The people of Israel were brokenhearted over their sin. It is time for us as the church to be brokenhearted as well, over our sin of covering and enabling sexual abuse.

There is a time to mourn, and that time is now. In many ways, we as the people of God have failed the weakest and most vulnerable among us. We need to cry out to God to have mercy on us all as we seek the way back to Him in repentance and faith, showing love to the oppressed in our midst. Let us pray that God will restore us and remake us in the image of Christ to love them and do whatever is necessary to accomplish the love and justice of God here in His church as much as His Spirit empowers us to do. Let us cry out to God that our churches won't be the ones with Ichabod written over the doorposts.[182]

> May we be people who are governed by God's Spirit, continually reliant on his leading. May we live among the facts of God's Word, transformed by and obedient to its truth. May we also learn to live among human facts, not hiding behind fortresses of theories and principles, but being willing like Jesus to get down into the midst of sickness, torment, and disease. It is only as the church of God manifests these characteristics that the life of God will be demonstrated in a redemptive way![183]

---

182   This is an allusion to 1 Samuel 4:21, implying that the glory of God has departed from the churches.

183   Langberg, *Counseling Survivors of Sexual Abuse*, pp. 277-278.

CHAPTER 11

WHAT THE OFFENDER MUST DO

This is perhaps the most difficult section of this book. What are the answers for offenders? How do we know they are truly repentant? Can they ever be trusted again? Do they have to leave the ministry? Will everything go back to normal?

THE HARD FACTS

Statistics show that change isn't easy

Recently our local paper ran a story about a man in his eighties who was arrested for molesting a child. A month or two later, a man in his nineties was arrested for the same thing. Believe it or not, that same year, a hundred-year-old man was released from prison after serving his sentence for child sexual abuse. He said he wanted to see his grandchildren and great-grandchildren and tell them he had done nothing wrong, but a short time later he was arrested again.

In our Speaking Truth in Love presentations, we use the results of different studies to show the extent of this sin. Dr. Anna Salter says, "In all the interviews I have done, I cannot remember one offender who did not admit privately to more victims than those for whom he had been caught. On the contrary, most offenders had been charged with and/or convicted of from one to three victims. In the interviews I have done, they have admitted to roughly 10 to 1,250 victims."[184] Most offenders are entrenched in this evil and very devious lifestyle, complete with all the hypocrisy, lying, manipulation, and even downright sociopathy that it necessitates. This set of attributes makes it difficult for the people of God to ascertain whether or not he truly has repented.

Second Corinthians 7:10 tells us, "For godly sorrow produces repentance leading to salvation, not to be regretted; but the sorrow of the world produces death." Enablers will often talk about how sorry offenders are, and of course most offenders will claim the same, but from what we have seen, read, and heard, many offenders are sorry only that they were caught or sorry that their ministry is in jeopardy or that they are being inconvenienced by the victim's pursuit of justice. This is not godly sorrow at all.

We need a miracle

A mother told us that when she confronted her husband about his molestation of their daughter, he repented on his knees, crying and begging for forgiveness. But some time later, the daughter found a camera in the bathroom that the father had been using to videotape her in the shower.

The alcoholic who is losing his marriage, his job, and his life needs divine intervention. The offender who has lived a two-faced lifestyle of secretly sexually violating the vulnerable needs a miracle

---

184   Salter, *Predators,* pp. 13-14.

too. If it were not for Matthew 19:26, which says, "With men this is impossible, but with God all things are possible," we may be tempted to lose hope for real change from offenders. But because we trust that God is the worker of miracles, we lay out five steps for restoration for the sexual abuse offender.

HE MUST MAKE A TRUE CONFESSION

"Dale, guess what I just got in the mail." It was my brother-in-law on the phone.

"What?" I asked. It was anybody's guess. The past few days, with Faith's father's crime against his foster granddaughter being found out, had been nearly crazy.

"A letter from a lawyer. Dad's lawyer."

"Oh no," I groaned. We had heard that he got a lawyer instead of going to the police, and even that Faith's mom had encouraged him to do it. "What does it say?"

"It says that if Alyssa gets up on the stand, she'll be sorry she did."

Here was more evidence, if we needed any more, that any show of repentance was a lie. The display of confession and repentance had all been a complete sham.

Jesus told His listeners in Matthew 5:23–24 that if they brought a gift to the altar and remembered that someone had something against them, they were to go make it right first and then come bring their gift. An offender cannot be right with God until he has done all he can to make things right with those he has sinned against.

Proverbs 28:13 says, "He who covers his sins will not prosper, but whoever confesses and forsakes them will have mercy." The offender who refuses to openly agree with God about his sin has God's mercy removed from him.

James 5:16 says, "Confess your trespasses to one another." If an offender apologizes with the intent of silencing the victim, he is not making a true confession. If he admits his sin but then blames others, he is not making a true confession. If he continues to minimize and excuse his actions, he is not making a true confession. If he rejects discipline or gets angry at the mention of consequences, he is not making a true confession. If he confesses to one but tells a different story to another, then this lying and covering is an indication that he still is not ready to acknowledge his sin and begin the lengthy process of dealing with it.

David said in Psalm 32:5, "I acknowledged my sin to you, and my iniquity I have not hidden." A true confession means that the offender agrees with God about the heinous nature of his sin, openly confessing it before the law, counselors, victims, victims' families, his own family, and the church. To show that his confession is real, it must be open, giving the truth to all who ask. This kind of transparency indicates a true confession.

A true and sincere apology that accompanies a true confession, showing deep sorrow and compassion for the victim while at the same time showing a willingness to change and bear the consequences, can be an instrument of great healing for all involved. When sexual assault survivors hear their offender publicly confess his great crime against them, this will help them in replacing lies with truth.

HE MUST BEAR FRUITS OF REPENTANCE

Going the other way

In Matthew 3:7-8, John the Baptist said to the most two-faced men of the New Testament, the Pharisees and Sadducees, "Brood of vipers! Who warned you to flee from the wrath to come? Therefore bear fruits worthy of repentance." Instead of hiding behind good works or heritage or appearance, those vipers who have committed the worst of hypocrisies must bring forth fruits worthy of repentance, turning and going the other way, having come to their senses that the way they were going was wrong.

Jeremiah 42 tells the story of the Israelites swearing before God that whatever God told them to do, they would do. Then, when God spoke through the prophet Jeremiah to tell them what to do, they decided they didn't like it and chose a way that was different from the one God had commanded. As a result of this lying, broken promise, and disobedience, most of them were destroyed.

The same will be true of offenders who promise to change but return to their old ways. Offenders and enablers are often quick to claim repentance and then demand that the victim forgive them, but often they lack the very prerequisite for repentance: a broken heart over their evil and the crimes they have committed.

Hebrews 12:16-17 talks about a "fornicator or profane person like Esau, who for one morsel of food sold his birthright. For you know that afterward, when he wanted to inherit the blessing, he was rejected, for he found no place for repentance, though he sought it diligently with tears." Esau was angry at missing the blessing, but he had no remorse for his sin that led to the loss. The religious sexual offender who thinks he can shed a few tears so that everything will be forgiven and forgotten is sadly mistaken.

From the statistics we've read and the stories we've heard, it seems that very few offenders ever truly repent. Hebrews 6:4–6 says, "For it is impossible for those who were once enlightened, and have tasted the heavenly gift, and have become partakers of the Holy Spirit, and have tasted the good word of God and the powers of the age to come, if they fall away, to renew them again to repentance since they crucify again for themselves the Son of God, and put Him to an open shame." Sexual abuse offenders who have claimed to be a Christian and have pretended Christianity with grandiose and even breathtaking hypocrisy, have so despised the good work of God that they had better be greatly afraid indeed.

So how do we know when an offender is repentant? Not when he says he is sorry, not when he sheds a few tears. It is when he turns his life from sin and back to following God. Repentance is not just saying a few words. It is a complete change of heart and behavior, going in a different direction, knowing that the old direction was wrong.

The appropriateness of shame

> "Dale, why are you being so harsh?"
>
> I was getting that question or some variant of it a good bit these days. "What are you referring to, Mrs. Morton?"
>
> "Well, you're saying that Faith's dad needs to go back and find all his victims from the past and make things right with them. But that's really asking too much, because that's all so long ago. That's under the blood."

"With God a thousand years is as a day," I countered. "It doesn't matter if his crimes were fifty years ago, he still needs to make them right. They'll be under the blood if he has truly repented, but he still needs to make them right with the people involved. And I don't see any evidence that he has any interest in doing that. He still laughs and jokes with everybody as if everything is just the same as ever. He talks about how he's being persecuted and didn't really do anything that bad. I don't see any shame."

After David's sin of adultery and murder, his shame was obvious to all. Besides his uncontrollable crying for days, he also went without food. The consequences of David's sin were harsh, but David accepted the consequences and took responsibility for what he had done. This acceptance showed that his repentance was real.

So what is the difference between David and Esau? Esau's remorse was over what he had missed out on. David's remorse was over his sin and the damage it caused.

Yes, an offender can repent and can be forgiven. Second Peter 3:9 says that the Lord "is longsuffering toward us, not willing that any should perish but that all should come to repentance." But Acts 26:20 says that the repentant one should "do works befitting repentance." God demands evidence in the life and works of those who claim it. Godly sorrow and true repentance must be verified over time.

HE MUST ACCEPT THE CONSEQUENCES OF HIS SIN

It goes against human nature to humbly accept the consequences of our deeds. But as we saw in chapter 7, consequences are a part of God's plan for dealing with sin. When our churches refuse to hold offenders accountable, they are standing not only against the oppressed and defenseless, but also against God.

If the offender is repentant, he will accept and even seek out the consequences placed on him from the law, church, and family, not try to avoid them. Although this is one of the hardest things that he must do, following through with consequences is vital.

Legal consequences

Though our justice system is a flawed one, many strides have been made in the last forty years to help victims of sexual abuse. Repentant offenders should turn themselves in to be punished by the legal system (Romans 13), and in recent times that has come to include not only serving time in prison, but also being put on a sex offender registry.

I knew a pastor who had molested two boys from his church. When he was caught and charged with the crime, he made a full confession, which meant confessing to more than what he had been charged with. He told me that the judge had called him a fool for confessing to the other offenses, but he wanted to be right before God and others. He is serving twelve years in prison, and last I knew, he was writing a curriculum for repentant offenders. I pray that someday God will use him as a force for good against this evil.

Protection for the vulnerable

The fact that a sexual abuse offender should never be around children cannot be stressed enough. Aside from any legal restrictions, a truly repentant offender will humbly accept the consequences of his abuse that affect his freedom of movement that, ideally, a licensed sex-offender counselor recommends. He will humbly comply with the stipulations drawn up by a church as outlined in chapter 10.

Will he humbly follow through?

If an offender won't graciously accept the boundaries that must be imposed as a result of his own criminal behavior, then this is an indication that he is not repentant and not sincere about going on the right road.

After Cain killed Abel, he received a just punishment from God but cried out, "My punishment is greater than I can bear!"[185] Actually, anything less than death was a mercy of God, and Cain should have understood that. Just as with murder, when someone rapes and molests, the punishment should be very severe for this terrible violation of a person, and one who is truly repentant will accept that.

HE MUST LABOR TO MAKE RESTITUTION

A different matter from punishment

Punishment and restitution are two different things. I remember a time when I was about six, when I was unhappy with the half banana my mom gave me, so I took my sister's half as well. When my mom caught me, she punished me. Later that day, when she gave out snacks, she gave my snack to my sister. Even though I had been punished, I still needed to make restitution.

For the most part, restitution is a lost concept today, but it was taught in God's Word as a principle to live by. In Exodus 22:1, God talks about this precept: "If a man steals an ox or a sheep, and slaughters

---

185 Genesis 4:13.

it or sells it, he shall restore five oxen for an ox and four sheep for a sheep." It is not enough simply to stop the sin of assaulting people sexually, but offenders must begin doing what is right. This is in line with the same principle presented in Ephesians 4:28: " Let him who stole steal no longer, but rather let him labor, working with his hands what is good, that he may have something to give him who has need."

Even though he could never repay

Luke 19:8 shows Zacchaeus feeling so convicted about his sin that he said, "If I have taken anything from anyone by false accusation, I restore fourfold." Zacchaeus knew that he needed not only to return anything he had stolen, but to restore four times as much according to the Old Testament stipulation.

This story is talking about material goods, which are relatively straightforward to reimburse. A sexual violation of a person's self, however, can never be "reimbursed." Most victims and their families would never want the offender to think that a monetary restitution somehow could make up for what he has done. No financial or material gift can make up for or repair the damage the offender has done.

However, there are a number of practical ways offenders can make honest restitution. They can pay sacrificially into a church fund for counseling and medical help for abuse survivors. They can sacrificially fund nonprofit ministries that cry out against this evil. They can speak publicly about the evil they have done and warn others not to go down the same road.

Does this seem like requiring too much? Think again about the violated ones who have survived to live lives of continual nightmares and flashbacks, self-hatred and shame, whose innocence, sense of self and safety, and even understanding of God was stolen by a lustful, controlling, and in some cases sadistic offender. It is not requiring too much.

HE MUST UNDERSTAND THAT RESTORATION IS NOT "RESET"

Offender reset button?

Just like the reset button restores a computer's previous settings, some offenders think that after they have said they're sorry and enough time has passed, that the clock should be reset and they can now sing in the choir, interact with children, teach Bible study, and go back to the way things were.

As I looked back over the years, I realized that's exactly what most of the family and church folks had always done. Some people would be angry and upset for a time and then after a few months or a year or two, all the concern would die down, things would go back the way they were, and every one would let down their guard again. Maybe it was because they really didn't know how to handle it, but without any repentance, confession, or restitution, they would simply "reset" the offender back to his previous "settings," before his sin was revealed. Nothing had changed, but everyone put their blindfolds back on and acted as if everything were the same as before.

We've sometimes heard from abuse survivors that they now have a "wonderful" relationship with their offender. By this they mean that they simply don't talk about the past. In most of these cases there was no dealing with the sin, no fruits of repentance, usually not even any seeking forgiveness. In other words, there was no real change; everything just went back to the way it was before. I cringe when I hear of victims of sexual abuse being reconciled to their offender, because very often the reality is that while the offenders may have convinced their family, church, and victims of their repentance and sincerity, they are often still molesting other children.

Hypocritical, two-faced viper offenders have lived all these years for power, control, and manipulation, and often the "reset" button is simply the way gullible people play the offender's game, which the offender always wins. Confession, repentance, acceptance of consequences, and an effort to make restitution should all precede the final step of restoration.

The final step

Restoration happens after the offender has gone through all the previous steps. Now Christians can eat and fellowship with him because he has made a full and godly confession, demonstrated that he has truly repented, has accepted all of the consequences of the sin, and is doing everything he can to make restitution. It means he may be able to attend an adults-only church service and a small group for adults. (He must not be allowed to have contact with children.)

If an offender is truly repentant and open about his sin, God can use him to help other offenders come to a place of true confession and true repentance as well. There is a great need for offenders who have a clear view of their sin and who are humbled before God, like the pastor who is now serving twelve years in prison, to reach out to other offenders and through tough love and biblical guidelines to help them turn from the way they were going and go the right way.

There is no shortcut on this road. All shortcuts will lead to failure and more abuse. But even though the confession, fruits of repentance, acceptance of the consequences, and restitution must be made before other people, the offender who truly puts his faith in Jesus Christ can trust that if he has confessed and repented before God (which will be obvious before others), he is without condemnation in Christ Jesus. In Romans 7:24-8:1 the Apostle Paul cried out, "O wretched man that I am! Who will deliver me from this body of death? I thank God—through Jesus Christ our Lord! . . . There is therefore now no condemnation to those who are in Christ Jesus."

The greatest hope of all for every believer, as well as the believer who is an offender, is that one day we will be rid of this old body and will be made whole without sin. For those of us who are in Christ, one day there will be no sin, no sinful thought, and we will all be perfect before Him, without fault or flaw.

CHAPTER 12

HOW FAMILY AND FRIENDS MUST HELP

What is the answer for the family of the victim, ones who are not enablers and want to provide the best possible care for their loved ones who have been sexually assaulted?

ENCOURAGE AN ENVIRONMENT OF OPEN COMMUNICATION

I remember as a teen having serious conversations with two friends on the risk of one of them, who was being abused by her father, being removed from the home, having to leave our Christian school and church and youth group. We talked many hours about this but didn›t know who we could trust. I carefully tried to ask my principal's wife at school some advice about this, for my friend. She thought I was talking about my dad and also started asking about which friend and got all nosy. If I had felt like I could trust her, I would have also told her about my own abuse. Instead she scared me off, and my friends and I came up with prevention strategies

to keep her dad out of her room and how she could sneak to the
bathroom at night.[186]

If we're going to be able to protect the vulnerable people in our
midst, we must have healthy and open lines of communication with
them. Patrick Crough says in *The Serpents Among Us*, "[W]e must make
it a point to communicate with our children every day to learn what is
going on in their lives and who they are having daily contact with."[187]
If family members and church members are truly connected with
each other on deep levels, then there will be far less vulnerability.

We must not turn a blind eye to suspicious behavior or signals
of distress that a child or even adult may be trying to send. We must
not only protect our most vulnerable but be open to hearing a report,
even if it's one we don't want to hear.

REPORT AN ALLEGATION OF ABUSE?

If the victim is a child

Author Victoria Johnson says in her book *Children and Sexual
Abuse*, "If sexual abuse has occurred, your main concern should be for
the victim. If you suspect, or your child reports, a sexual encounter,
allow the child to explain what happened. Stay as calm as possible.
Don't get angry or blame the child. Believe your child. . . . Rarely do
children make up sexual abuse stories."[188]

All that is necessary for evil to triumph is for good men to do nothing.
No matter how nice, helpful, good-looking, honest, pleasant, sincere,

---

186   Personal correspondence, used by permission.
187   Patrick Crough, *The Serpents Among Us*, p. 254.
188   Johnson, *Children and Sexual Abuse*, p. 10.

powerful, or innocent the accused person may seem, if a child has given you a disclosure of abuse, report it to the legal authorities. Don't wait for the pastor to do it. Care more for the safety of your child than for what people will think about you. When family members and even friends and church members report the abuse to the police rather than trying to handle the matter themselves, this helps the authorities be able to do their job more effectively, reassuring the alleged victims that the family will be looking out for their safety. If the offender is a family member or primary breadwinner, this decision may be a very difficult one, but it's still necessary.[189]

If the one who was abused is telling for the first time as an adult

Though statutes of limitations on the crime of sexual abuse are changing around the country to be extended or eliminated altogether, they still vary by state. Even if this particular case is past the statute of limitations, the one who was violated may want to report it for a number of reasons. Most offenders have many victims, so alerting the authorities to the fact of the abuse could be of help in future cases, and could even help prosecute the offender on a more recent case by being a witness. However, the process of reporting can in itself be very traumatizing for abuse survivors, and the people in their lives should not push them to report but should support them no matter what decision they make about whether or not to report.

---

189   This is an ideal opportunity for other family members and our churches to support the devastated family of the offender in order to help them as they seek to attain financial stability.

SURROUND THE VICTIM WITH PROTECTION

For the disclosing child

When a child has been violated, once the legal authorities have been notified, social services will become involved and will help you decide what will be in the best interest of the child. Instead of blaming and shaming victims, the family must give love and support, forming a circle of protection and affirmation, assuring victims that they were not to blame.

Some parents have told us that their child no longer talks with them because the parents failed to properly respond to the child's cries for help. For example, a mother told us that when her son disclosed his molestation by an older cousin, the father said it was no big deal. If a parent refuses to protect their child, then they have failed to do what God has entrusted them to do. Be a protector, not a pretender. Don't ignore the obvious, closing your eyes and ears to the cries of the vulnerable, pretending everything is all right. Instead, see the danger and come to the aid of the wounded one.

When the victim is disclosing as an adult survivor

If you are a loving and caring friend, don't be surprised if a friend chooses to disclose his or her abuse to you. The abused are all around us; remember that statistics tell us that one in four women and one in six men will be abused by the age of eighteen. These statistics don't even include the abuses that can happen to adults, especially in the military and in college.[190] In the case of the adult survivors of abuse,

---

190   For example, see Jesse Ellison, "The Military's Secret Shame," Newsweek, April 3, 2011, accessed via https://swilliamsjd.wordpress.com/2011/04/08/the-military%E2%80%99s-secret-shame-%E2%80%93by-jesse-ellison-newsweek. See also the Washington Post article "Sexual assault on campus: Getting a clearer

the sense of protection is given through your surrounding them with love and help and assurance that you stand with them against the evil. "What we need to tell the victim early on is that what has happened to them [sic] is wicked and evil in God's sight, and that God is against wicked men who do this. . . .. After making it clear that God is against the sin of abuse and the sole blame lies with the perpetrator, we then need to assure her that God is actively for her, and we are for her too. We are against the evil man."[191]

LISTEN WITH HUMILITY

When seemingly respectable people are accused of sexual abuse, many will use their voices to rally to their defense. But one of the most important questions we face in understanding sexual abuse is this: Who will listen to the voices of the victims? "How little value we place on listening! To attend to the struggle of another by listening is to bestow honor on that person."[192]

Listen when they can't speak of it

Faith recounts that even as a pastor's wife, if someone had asked her if she had ever been sexually abused, she probably would have said no, because the pain and embarrassment were just too great. In fact, until 2005, I was the only one Faith had told about her abuse.

---

picture," November 2, 2014, accessed via http://www.washingtonpost.com/opinions/sexual-assault-on-campus-getting-a-clearer-picture/2014/11/02/2f16166a-611b-11e4-8b9e-2ccdac31a031_story.html.

191   Crippen and Wood, *A Cry for Justice*, p 215. Because they write about domestic abuse, Crippen and Wood speak of victims as primarily women, but we know that victims of sexual abuse include boys and men.

192   Langberg, *Counseling Survivors of Sexual Abuse*, p. 280.

The reasons a survivor keeps that wall of silence up, sometimes for decades, often go back to the reasons the victim didn't speak in the first place—usually terrifying fear and crippling shame. One male survivor put it this way:

> The very hardest part of recovery for me was coming out and saying that I am a sexually abused person. I didn't know until two years ago that men and boys could be raped. We're not supposed to be victims.[193]

There may come a point when you know your friend has been abused but know little else. Be willing to sit with him or her in grief without needing to know details. One abuse survivor wrote:

> It is so hard to talk about the abuse, never mind share it with someone for the first time. The first time I told anyone was to a high school counselor. I told her about my brother first because he was coming home from Navy boot camp, and I was afraid. I then slipped in that my dad was doing the same sorts of things to me. Later that day, I was called into her office to find my parents sitting there laughing and carrying on. My dad, a prominent man in our small town, made me sit on his lap in front of the counselor and said, "Now you know I would never hurt you! I love you!"
>
> I wanted to throw up.
>
> The next meeting with the counselor was with my brother, and me—alone. He confessed and cried. She called it "experimentation," and said she would not tell my parents what happened because this was between him and me, not him and them. We were

---

sent home with a bonding exercise to bake a cake together. We never spoke of it again.

I wasn't heard. I wasn't believed. No one reported my dad or my brother.

The first time someone really heard me was the time I slowly spoke three words: "They raped me." My friend sat in silence and held my hand. She waited patiently between my sobs and dissociation for any more words, but they did not come, and she did not require them. She sat with me and felt my pain with me. In the quiet, she reminded me that it wasn't my fault. She reminded me that this did not change one thing she thought about me. She still loved me, and so did Jesus. She believed me. She proved that, by continuing to meet with me and to love me. For many years after that, she prayed with me and for me. Later I learned that she felt my pain so easily because she had the same experiences as a child.[194]

Listen when they begin to speak

When a person has been through a deeply traumatic experience, though there may initially be an inability to speak about it, eventually a point may come where speaking about it becomes absolutely necessary. In the book *Invisible Girls,* Dr. Patti Feuereisen tells victims: "The most important thing you can do is simply tell someone, because telling is the beginning of healing."[195] When Faith began her healing process, she

---

194   Personal correspondence, used by permission.

195   Patti Feuereisen, *Invisible Girls: The Truth About Sexual Abuse* (Berkeley: Seal Press, 2002), p. 25. More than simply telling, healing must be facilitated by telling someone who will listen with compassion.

began to grow into the person that God had intended her to be all the time. Sadly, though, Faith's mom told her that she didn't want to hear about the abuse, and to this day she refuses to let Faith talk with her about the abuse. What a tragedy that is—she could have helped bring healing by listening and showing sorrow and compassion.

Sometimes abuse survivors aren't ready to talk about their abuse until years or even decades after the trauma has occurred. When you develop meaningful relationships, you can show love that can bring a survivor to feel that it's safe to speak when he or she is ready. When survivors first begin to speak years after the event, they may ask you not to disclose their abuse-survivor identity to anyone, because they are still coming to terms with it themselves. Keep their confidences as they continue to find their own voices.[196]

Listen when they can speak of little else

Retelling the story can be a necessary part of processing the trauma of sexual abuse. In her article "Coping with Traumatic Memory," Christian psychologist Dr. Diane Langberg says,

> Survivors will say the same things over and over—"I saw the color of their ties." They will be repetitious in dealing with their emotions—"I am so angry that . . ." And they will repeat their losses again and again—"I cannot believe

---

196   Abuse survivors may agonize over whether telling about their abuse would violate appropriate boundaries, whether certain details of sadism or violence would simply be gratuitous, or a number of other related issues. Though these matters can't be addressed in this book, other books can be helpful, such as Diane Langberg's *Counseling Survivors of Sexual Abuse*. The most important thing to remember, always, as you listen, is that genuine love and grief and righteous anger are always appropriate. Shaming and blaming the abuse survivor are not.

so-and-so is dead." Expect it and learn to sit with it. The magnitude of the trauma is so great that repetition is necessary. The mind cannot imagine what happened. It cannot hold such a thought. Bearing the intensity of emotions is impossible, and so the feelings must be tried on again and again. These are attempts to bear what cannot be born [sic]. They are struggles to integrate into life what does not fit, for there are not categories. Be patient and then be patient some more.[197]

The abuse victim's voice was silenced through the initial crime; it may well have been silenced again by abuse enablers, whether devious or well-meaning. Now, to speak the truth about what actually happened to someone who will accept the story and show compassion will be the most important step for the survivor to be able to tear down the wall of silence. The speaking, in and of itself, will restore a measure of self-worth to a valuable soul who was stripped of all self-worth. Receiving the story with compassion will show value for souls who thought of themselves as valueless. Grieving with survivors will show love for those who may have thought of themselves as unworthy of love.

Listen when they have questions you can't answer

Even though we as Christians believe in the existence of great evil—else why would Jesus have to die?—coming face to face with great evil may bring a sense of trauma to our own souls. Resist the

---

197   Diane Langberg, Ph.D., "Coping with Traumatic Memory," *Marriage and Family: a Christian Journal.* 5(4), pp. 447-456.

urge to protect your soul through quickly deflecting the hard questions with a pat answer. Run to Jesus instead.

> Sitting with an [abuse] survivor brings you face to face with the sickest, most twisted and evil things human beings do to each other. . . . Many men and women have lived in terrible isolation, thinking their secrets were too horrible to be told. Calling back memories that one has never been able to voice is a massive struggle. Hearing about such things can cause great denial in the listener. Yet we who believe that sin is so hideous as to require the death of God himself should, of all people, find evil believable.[198]

Jeff Crippen, speaking of domestic abuse, asks a question that is every bit as pertinent to the friends of sexual abuse survivors: "Are *you* willing? Would you listen to her story with compassion, and listen again and yet again as she chooses to tell you more? Would you refrain from giving knee-jerk advice?"[199] This last question highlights once again the need for humility in listening. Oh, how much we wish for easy answers for the pain and horror. But the easy answers we can give ("Trust God. He has his reasons. He was there. He loves you. Jesus cares; you are valuable")—as true as they are!—can sound like platitudes to one who is deeply wounded, especially if those words were used as part of the abuse. This is why it's so necessary to listen with humility and seek the leading of the Holy Spirit as we walk with someone who is healing. He is the one who can help the abuse

---

198   Langberg, *Counseling Survivors of Sexual Abuse*, pp. 279-280.

199   Crippen and Wood, *A Cry for Justice*, p 211.

survivor remove the lies that have been embedded in the soul and replace them with the truth.

Even when you have no words, your facial expressions and body language can communicate condemnation or compassion. Don't underestimate the power of unspoken words. One abuse survivor wrote to a friend:

> *Instead of using the Bible to guilt me into being different, it seems you are living a picture of Jesus before me. What I am struggling to see in him, you are showing me by what you do, by how you act, how you respond, etc. always patient when things aren't connecting and making sense. I guess, in a way, I am really seeing a different picture—perhaps a more realistic picture of who God is. I see him in you and others at church. He seems to be using those who are a reflection of himself to point me to who he is.*[200]

This is what family and friends can do. As we tear down the wall of silence and secrecy surrounding sexual violence, we can listen and love well. By our actions as much as our words, we can offer hope and encouragement.

LOVE THEM WELL

Be willing to show love in small ways

We can't always know how deeply a small act of kindness can affect an abuse survivor. One survivor talked about how deeply she was touched that a man in the church would care enough about her to walk her to her car in the dark, because her father would never have done such a thing. A survivor who had engaged in self-harm was

---

200 Personal correspondence, used by permission.

overwhelmed by the love her friends showed simply by sending her pictures of butterflies. Another abuse survivor said:

> *When I was in the pit of despair, a friend asked me quietly if she could pray for me, and I nodded yes. She took gentle hold of my hand and began to pray the sweetest prayer, telling Jesus how special I was to her, and how broken I was. She prayed for me as she would pray for her child, in a very loving and precious way. She still doesn't know how she touched me that night, just by being there, holding my hand and praying. She still doesn't know of the abuse, but she has taken care to check in on me, ask me how I am and if she can do anything to encourage me. She has taken me out to coffee, given me words of encouragement by occasional texts and cards. She loved me and has shown that over and over without needing to know any details of my brokenness.*[201]

Turning an abuse survivor into your personal project—seeing him or her as a task to be accomplished or a broken thing to be fixed—is *not* loving well. It's vital for followers of Jesus to see abuse survivors as they are: our equals, made in the image of God, chosen and beloved by Him.

Be willing to be uncomfortable

No matter how uncomfortable it is for you, no matter how shocking and sickening, don't make the mistake of cutting the abuse survivor off from speaking about it. As you come face to face with real evil and breathtaking hypocrisy, fall flat on your face in utter dependence

---

201   Personal correspondence, used by permission.

on your Savior Jesus Christ and continue to show the compassion that He shows. Open your heart to the abuse survivor whenever he or she is ready to speak, to listen and receive the story and to grieve a tragedy that may never before have been properly grieved.

Dan Allender, in *The Wounded Heart,* speaks directly to friends of sexual abuse survivors.

> You are the friend of someone who has been abused, and you are untrained, inexperienced, and scared. If I am accurate so far, then you have also seriously thought about backing out of the relationship with your abused friend. Not that you are going to treat her like a leper or avoid all contact, but the issue of abuse, the current struggles and fears, are off limits.
>
> My counsel to you is simple: Don't back off from the frightening terrain of a wounded heart. You may say the wrong things and even cause more harm, but the worst harm is to turn your back. Accept your limitations, but also acknowledge the fact that you are on the front lines of the battle. You may not like to hear it, but the fact is you are a foot soldier, an infantryman who is often the first to take the fire of the enemy.
>
> As a therapist, I see your friend once or maybe twice a week. You see her every day. I deal with significant issues in her soul, but you talk about the same issues, and even more. I may be necessary to the process, but you are even

more so. . . . Don't allow your inexperience or your own personal past to keep you from loving well.[202]

Be willing to walk the long journey of healing

Healing from the deep trauma and scarring of abuse will not necessarily happen quickly. Though God sometimes does heal miraculously, more often healing is a long road.

The allegory *Hinds' Feet on High Places* tells the story of little lame Much Afraid and her journey with the Shepherd to the High Places. On the way, she has to take detours, turn the opposite direction from the way she wants to go, struggle through desert, forest, and flood. Often Much Afraid despairs that she will never reach her destination. Again and again the Good Shepherd encourages her that every place he leads her in her road of healing is to grow her in strength and draw her to himself so that she will find her greatest joy and fulfillment in Him.[203]

With confidence we can know that full healing can come through Jesus Christ. As we point abuse survivors to Him, we'll be able to rejoice as we see them become victors and in turn reach out their hands to help others on their healing journey.

One mother wrote:

> *The last seven years of our lives have been gut-wrenching. Three of our daughters were molested, and one of my precious girls has turned to a lesbian lifestyle. She is very unhappy and feels alone. We are working with her and loving her and are just plain patient*

---

202   Allender, *The Wounded Heart*, pp. 235-236.

203   Hannah Hurnard, *Hinds' Feet on High Places* (Colchester, UK: Christian Literature Crusade, 1955).

with her. I really think God will heal her one day. I have learned to reach through the flames and love my daughter.[204]

Shortly after writing this, this mother and her husband witnessed a prodigal-daughter gift of return. The road of recovery will still be a long one, but to walk with an abuse survivor on the road to recovery is a high calling. "There is no shortcut for dealing with human beings and their difficulties. God is a living Spirit; the Word is living and alive; the Spirit indwells living souls, who in turn are ministering to other living souls."[205]

This is as it should be. This is the body of Christ at work.

SPEAK OUT

In the old Dr. Seuss classic *Horton Hears a Who,* Horton was the only one who could hear the cries of the many people in the tiny city on the clover blossom. To convince others of their existence, he encouraged them in their chant, "We are here. We are here! We are here!" Finally the chant grew loud enough to break through the invisible barrier of silence, and the doubters were able to hear the cry for help.

Even though the existence and number of victims of sexual abuse is staggering, the wall of silence that churches have erected has produced many doubters in the pews and even among the church leaders. The voices of victims, though, are crying out louder and louder, "We are here!" Like Horton, some of us who have heard the cries of these victims are speaking out to convince skeptical Christians that they need to deal with this heinous sin.

204 Personal correspondence, used by permission.
205 Langberg, *Counseling Survivors of Sexual Abuse,* p. 276.

During the shameful period of African slavery in the U.S. and England, God called some people to be a voice for the voiceless. William Wilberforce spoke out against slavery in the British Parliament for years before he saw any results. Harriet Beecher Stowe spoke out through her book, *Uncle Tom's Cabin,* one of the most widely read books of the entire nineteenth century. Many others spoke out in other ways. Some provided a platform for former slaves themselves to speak out.

Today, as more and more abuse survivors find their voices and speak out about their abuse, God will call more of us who were not abused to join them. Our speaking out doesn't have to be grandiose, in Parliament, or in a best-selling book. But we can speak to others in our churches and small groups, we can speak with family members and friends, helping them understand the horrors of abuse and the shame that falls on those of us who cover for it and blame the victims.

Follow hard after God. Seek Him and cry out to Him. Don't let Him go as you long to be a voice for the voiceless. He grants you the shield of faith in Jesus Christ, the breastplate of righteousness of Jesus Christ, the helmet of your salvation in Jesus Christ, your loins girded with the truth of Christ, and holding the sword of the Spirit, which is the Living Word of God.[206] In Him, we are empowered to do His work. For Him, for them, we can do no less.

---

206 Ephesians 6:10–18.

CHAPTER 13

THE ABUSE SURVIVOR'S SHEPHERD

What is the answer for those who have been victimized? How can you ever recover from the horrific experience of sexual assault? Does Jesus care? Will you ever be whole again? Will you ever be able to enjoy sexual intimacy with your husband or wife?

Your questions may be many and overwhelming. But you can have great hope.

UNDERSTAND THAT GOD IS GREAT: HE IS AT WORK IN SPITE OF THE EVIL OF MEN

What God says about His own work

In the book of Job, we read that Job's world was shattered in one day. Satan set in motion a series of events that would rob Job of everything he possessed and included the tragic death of his ten children. These things didn't happen to Job because of his sin—the Bible says that Job was a godly and an upright person. Instead, Satan desired to destroy Job and his testimony. Job was a victim. He suffered "at no fault of his own."

At first Job's reaction was amazingly accepting of God's will. He praised God and acknowledged God's authority over his life. But after another satanic attack of grievous illness that covered him with painful sores, he was forsaken by all who used to respect and admire him.

Finally Job cried out in his pain and agony, cursing the day he was born and expressing the grief that he felt. He complained! He lamented. He was depressed, suicidal, and angry. Eventually Job began questioning why God had brought all the suffering into his life. He pointed out to God that he had done nothing wrong or deserving of such evil circumstances.

Just as there was no sin in Job's life that caused the calamities that befell him, it is not the sin of the victim that causes sexual abuse. It is because of the evil of the perpetrator and because of sin in the world in general. We live in a sinful and fallen world, a world where horrible things happen to many people every day.

After many chapters of Job's pleading with God to give him an answer explaining why all these things happened to him, to Job's great surprise, God appeared to speak with him personally. It would seem that finally Job was going to get some answers. But that's not what happened.

Instead God talked about Himself and His amazing creation. He talked about His wisdom and power and how He created and fashioned the whole earth, the water cycle, the sunrise, the springs at the bottom of the ocean, the treasury of snow and hail, lightning and thunder, the animals He created, with all of their strength, beauty, majesty, and grace, cunning, and speed.

For four chapters God never mentioned what Job had gone through; for four chapters, God answered none of Job's primary questions. God took Job's attention off his own problems and put it on God's greatness.

To someone who has gone through sexual abuse or great pain and suffering, God's response to Job may seem offensive, but hear what Job said in chapter 42: "I know that you can do everything, and that no purpose of yours can be withheld from you. You asked 'who is this that darkens council without knowledge?' Therefore I have uttered what I did not understand, things too wonderful for me, which I did not know. Listen, please and let me speak, you said 'I will question you and you shall answer me.' Then Job said 'I have heard of you by the hearing of the ear. But now my eye sees you, therefore I abhor myself [turn from my former way of thinking] and repent in dust and ashes.'"

God guided Job's eyes away from himself and pointed them toward God, His great works, and His greater purpose. He gave Job an amazing picture of the promise of eternity yet to come. Job no longer needed to lament, because God redirected his eyes. He no longer asked questions like "why?" or "why me?" or "where were you, God?" Even though Job didn't receive answers to any of his original questions, this vision of God in all His glory changed Job's life.

If God were to give you answers to explain why you have gone through abuse, they wouldn't take away the pain and the longing you have inside. What will help transform your life and give it meaning, purpose, and peace is for you to see God for who He is. Then the need to know answers to your questions will begin to lose their power over you.

The book of Job . . . does not present a path of wisdom and patience that is for super-holy Christians. The book of Job is nothing less than the gospel of Jesus Christ. It is the good news that God comes for his people, but he does not come on our terms. He does not come and leave us untouched or unchanged. He comes to transfigure us—to cleanse us, transform us, and draw us up into his glorious presence. He comes in the storm of his presence, and he blows upon us and our families and our stories; he blows upon them until they glow with the fire of his glory. The act of reading and studying the book of Job is an invitation into that storm. It is a call to enter the whirlwind, to walk into the hurricane of his glory.[207]

What God says about the evil of men

When Samuel approached a young man that he was sure must be destined to be the next king of Israel, God said, "Do not look at his appearance or at his physical stature, because I have refused him. For the Lord does not see as man sees; for man looks at the outward appearance, but the Lord looks at the heart."[208] God knew that no matter how "kingly" the young man before him appeared, his heart was not toward the Lord. Similarly, in spite of what might be a near-perfect outward appearance, God knows the evil in the hearts of sexual offenders. He is not overlooking their evil.

The prophet Ezekiel reported, "God said to me, have you seen what the elders of the house of Israel do in the dark, every man in the

---

207   Toby J. Sumpter, *Job Through New Eyes: A Son for Glory* (Monroe, LA: Athanasius Press, 2012), p. vi.

208   1 Samuel 16:7.

room of his idols? For they say, the Lord does not see us."[209] The religious leaders tried to convince themselves that God would not see all the evil they were doing in the darkness. But He sees, and He knows.

In Ezekiel chapter 34, God spoke some harsh words for the leaders of Israel, the ones He called "shepherds," who weren't really taking care of the sheep:

> Woe to the shepherds of Israel who feed themselves!
>
> Should not the shepherds feed the flocks?
>
> You eat the fat and clothe yourselves with the wool;
>
> you slaughter the fatlings, but you do not feed the flock.
>
> The weak you have not strengthened, nor have you healed those who were sick,
>
> nor bound up the broken, nor brought back what was driven away, nor sought what was lost;
>
> but with force and cruelty you have ruled them.
>
> So they were scattered because there was no shepherd;
>
> and they became food for all the beasts of the field when they were scattered.
>
> My sheep wandered through all the mountains, and on every high hill;
>
> yes, My flock was scattered over the whole face of the earth,
>
> and no one was seeking or searching for them.

God then pronounced judgment on the wicked shepherds. Judgment is coming on evil men, especially religious leaders. Though God's judgment can seem very slow in coming, we can be confident that it will come.

UNDERSTAND THAT GOD IS GOOD: HE KNOWS YOU AND LOVES YOU

The Good Shepherd of Ezekiel 34

God pronounced judgment on the evil shepherds. Then he said:

Indeed I myself will search for my sheep and seek them out.

As a shepherd seeks out his flock on the day he is among his scattered sheep,

so will I seek out my sheep and deliver them from all the places

where they were scattered on a cloudy and dark day.

And I will bring them out from the peoples and gather them from the countries,

and will bring them to their own land;

I will feed them on the mountains of Israel,

in the valleys and in all the inhabited places of the country.

I will feed them in good pasture, and their fold shall be on the high mountains of Israel.

There they shall lie down in a good fold and feed in rich pasture on the mountains of Israel.

I will feed my flock, and I will make them lie down . . .

I will seek what was lost and bring back what was driven away, bind up the broken and strengthen what was sick;

but I will destroy the fat and the strong, and feed them in judgment.

The wicked ones who have abused the sheep will be brought to justice, and the sheep will be protected under the True Shepherd of their souls.

Out of the wilderness, out of the pit

Genesis 16 tells about Hagar the slave girl who was driven into the wilderness with her son, not knowing what to do or where to go, expecting to die, thinking that she was alone with no one to show her love or compassion. At her lowest point and in the moment of her deepest need, God met her and spoke to her, acknowledging her affliction and showing compassion for her. Then Hagar realized that God saw her—in her pain, suffering, and loneliness. She realized that God was meeting her, showing compassion, and giving her hope. God saw Hagar as someone who was precious and of great value.

Abuse survivors may have been told the lie that they are completely alone and that no one knows or cares about their abuse, and they may continue to believe this lie. Even children who are born as a result of sexual assault can struggle with who they are. But the truth is that God sees and knows and cares. The survivor of abuse or the child that is born out of sexual assault is loved by God and has been given a special purpose in life, just like everyone else. When God sees you, He doesn't just see what has happened to you, but He sees you for who you are as a person, and He knows the plans that He has for you. Many beautiful Scriptures offer hope for seeing ourselves as beloved in God's eyes, and can offer great comfort in times of meditation.

God sent the prophet Jeremiah to warn the people of Israel about their sin and the need to repent, but the people didn't listen. Finally, the lowest point in his life came when he was thrown into a dungeon where he "sank in the mire" so deep that he couldn't even move.[210] Even though he had done right, he was hated, mocked, ridiculed, and left to die in the stink and darkness of the dungeon.

Those who have been sexually abused may have been told the lie that the abuse has left them in shame and darkness. It can still feel like a dungeon from which they will never be able to escape. If God didn't protect them before, how can they trust him now?

But Jeremiah knew the truth—that only God truly had the answers to the sin and evil of this world. In Jeremiah's case, a man who loved God intervened and helped him get out of the pit. We pray that God will raise up many compassionate people who love Him and who will come alongside abuse survivors and walk with them as they, with the Lord's help, plant their feet on the Solid Rock of Jesus Christ.

God's love for you is great

Even with all the hardships Jeremiah endured, the book of Jeremiah contains some beautiful expressions of God's love.

> The Lord has appeared of old to me, saying:
> "Yes, I have loved you with an everlasting love;
> Therefore with lovingkindness I have drawn you."[211]

What happened to you was wicked, and God is outraged with the one who harmed you. Grief and anger and lament are appropriate.

---

210   Jeremiah 38:6.
211   Jeremiah 31:3.

But also remember that Jesus paid the ultimate sacrifice for you. When you ask, "Where was God when I was being abused?" you can be confident of His outrage at the abusers. But you can also remember, "He was on the cross." Jesus endured the pain and suffering of the cross two thousand years ago because of His love for you right now. Jesus told His disciples in John 15:13, "Greater love has no one than this, than to lay down one's life for his friends." Not long after Jesus said these words, He gave his life for us.

Psalm 23, the beautiful Shepherd psalm, is not just for other people. It is for *you*. The Lord is *your* Good Shepherd. He leads *you* beside still waters. He will restore *your* soul. When *you* walk through the valley of dark shadows, He will be with *you*. Read it with the confidence that the Shepherd of your soul loves *you*.

Abuse survivors may have been told the lie that they are unlovely, without value, guilty, and even unworthy, and they may still believe it. But Jesus said the truth in John 3:16: "For God so loved the world that he gave his only begotten Son, that whoever believes in him should not perish but have everlasting life." Every person is so important to God that He sent His dear Son to die for them. God wants you with Him for eternity so much so that He died for you. Jesus Christ did not die for "good" people, but He died for people who were wounded, lost, hurting, and in desperate need of Him.

In Psalm 139 the psalmist David lets us know the truth: each one of us is a marvelous creation, and God was involved in every detail of our creation. No matter how you think you may appear, you are very precious and marvelous in God's sight. We pray that you will come to see yourself as God sees you, as someone who is fearfully and wonderfully made.

UNDERSTAND WHAT JESUS CHRIST DID FOR YOU AND IS FOR YOU

He lived a perfect life and died a perfect death for you

God's demands of His people are huge and unreachable. If you try to meet the demands of God on your own, you are lost and hopeless. But the good news is that Jesus Christ, through His perfect life, fulfilled all of the law of God, not just for Himself, but for every person who puts faith and trust in Him. ALL of the demands of God's holy law are fulfilled. When you are in Christ, you no longer need to look to law-keeping (or even principle-following) to live a Christian life that is pleasing to God. Instead, in faith you can look to Christ.

Even though Jesus lived a perfect life, still He was beaten and scorned. The crown of thorns was driven deep into His scalp. His flesh was torn by whips. His body was so weakened by loss of blood that He didn't have the strength to carry His own cross. Nails were pounded into His hands and feet, and then He hung on the cross until He died.

Jesus said in John 12:32, "And I, if I am lifted up from the earth, will draw all peoples to myself." Jesus desires that His sacrifice for you on the cross will draw you to Himself. He wants to bring peace and love into your life.

He rose again for you

Jesus rose to gain victory over death for Himself at that time, which we all know well. But just as crucial, He rose *to gain victory over what may feel like a living death for you, here and now.* He did it to insure your own resurrection in Him today, so that when you look to Him in faith, you will walk in newness of life *by the power of His Spirit in you,* right here on this earth.

Ephesians 4 tells us that when He ascended to heaven, He "gave gifts to men,"[212] the most important of which was the Holy Spirit. When you trust in Christ, the Holy Spirit will empower you to take one step after another in your journey with your Shepherd.

Jesus wants to transform you out of your suffering and pain into a new life, a real life. He said in John 10:10, "The thief does not come except to steal, and to kill, and to destroy. I have come that they may have life, and that they may have it more abundantly."

He is . . .

If you have trusted in Him, Jesus Christ is so many things for you. These are just a few to meditate on. These verses don't constitute a take-two-verses-and-call-me-in-the-morning "solution" to your deepest questions. Rather, these are declarations about the Son of God that you can return to, again and again, with the prayer that a vital truth that the Living Word of God has to offer for your soul may become more real to you each time.

> *He is your Passover Sacrifice* (1 Corinthians 5:7). He was offered in your place, your substitute.

> *He is your Rescuer* (Titus 3:5–6). It is through His rescuing that you have been brought to a place of being washed and renewed.

---

212 Ephesians 4:8.

He is your Sin-washer (1 Corinthians 6:11). You are made clean and new in Him.

He is your Mediator (1 Timothy 2:5). It is because of Him alone that you can stand before God the Father.

He is your Redemption (1 Corinthians 1:30). Through Him you experience full release from the bondage of sin and shame of the past. Through Him you are set free.

He is your Righteousness (1 Corinthians 1:30). He has already accomplished everything that ever needs to be done. You can do nothing more to attain God's favor. Jesus has done it all!

He is your Sanctification (1 Corinthians 1:30). Farewell to a by-your-bootstraps Christian life! Welcome to a life of deep dependence on the One who is all your holiness!

He is your High Priest (Hebrews 4:20). Through the veil, His flesh, Jesus has made a new and living way into the very presence of God the Father. Because He is your High Priest, you can go in with boldness.

He is your Wisdom (1 Corinthians 1:30). You can look to Jesus in confidence that He will be your Guide.

He is your Strength (Exodus 15:2). In Him alone you are strong to do battle in the realm of the spirit.

He is your Joy (John 15:11). His "energizing delight" can abide in you, through the ability of His Spirit.

He is your Peace (Ephesians 2:14; John 16:33). He is your peace with God. He is your peace with others of all tribes and tongues and nations and languages. He is the peace-be-still within your soul.

He is your Vine (John 14). As the branch on the Vine, you can continually draw from His life. You don't have to be stuck trying to dredge up a Christian life of your own from nothing.

He is your Song (Exodus 15:2). And His love and glory, His holiness and tenderness, His righteousness and mercy, His many glorious attributes will give us themes for songs throughout eternity.

He is your Hope (1 Timothy 1:1). All your expectations, all your anticipation, rest in Him, with utter confidence of total fulfillment of all good things.

He is your Lord (2 Peter 3:18). By His very nature and by His wondrous accomplishments, Jesus stands in position to command you in every way.

He is your Good Shepherd (John 10:11). Jesus cares for you. He loves you. He calls you by name. He tenderly carries you and strengthens you.

UNDERSTAND WHO YOU ARE
WHEN YOU ARE IN CHRIST

The first step to healing begins with receiving Jesus Christ as your Lord and Savior, by faith trusting Him to rescue you and lead you as a gentle Shepherd. When you do, you can be sure that several wonderful things will be true about you. These beautiful truths can replace the lies imbedded by the abuser and the enemy of your soul.

You are His new, pure creation

People who have been abandoned and rejected by the ones who should have been caring for them may believe the lie that all they are is filthy and broken. One important truth to remember is that before trusting in Christ, everyone is in a state of brokenness and uncleanness before God.

When we accept Christ as our Savior, so many things change. We're encouraged by 2 Corinthians 5:17: "Therefore, if anyone is in Christ, he is a new creation; old things have passed away; behold, all things have become new." You are no longer a condemned, broken sinner but a new, pure creation. The final transformation will take place once we are with Him in heaven. Revelation 21:5 says, "Then he who sat on the throne said, 'Behold, I make all things new.'"

You are His beloved child

I remember when our five children were little, one of my favorite things to do was to hold them with their arms around my neck or their head on my shoulder. This was the most special feeling of love and being loved. Now I have three grandsons and a granddaughter, and I enjoy the same moments with them. Sometimes when my children were hurting, I went to bed crying because I hurt for them.

God loves us as His own children, and He wants us to love him back. Psalm 103:13 reminds us, "As a father pities [has compassion on] his children, so the Lord pities [has compassion on] those who fear him [have respect and reverence for him]." Jesus wept with compassion over Jerusalem because He wanted to protect them when they turned away from God. Jesus wept with compassion over His friend Lazarus's death. Jesus holds His children close and shows compassion on people who have been sexually abused.

Sometimes people have shared with us that their parents told them that they were a "mistake." The sense of abandonment caused by this can bring what feels like unbearable pain, hurt, and confusion. But the truth is that no child is an accident in God's eyes. Psalm 27:10 says, "When my father and my mother forsake me, then the Lord will take care of me."

In Ezekiel 16:1–6 we see a picture of a newborn baby who had been abandoned, filthy and naked, and left for dead. No one pitied the child or lifted a hand to help, but God loved the baby that had been despised, neglected, and abandoned. He carefully washed the baby and clothed and cared for it. He loved it and took it as His child. Even more in the New Testament, we see that when we trust in Christ, we are brought into the family of God. Galatians 3:26 says, "For you are all sons of God through faith in Christ Jesus."

Sadly, for many victims of sexual abuse, their families are angry or offended at them, repeating the lie that the victims have brought shame and embarrassment to the family name. But the truth is that God welcomes His children to bear His name. It is through Christ's name and faith in His name and all He has done for us that we are redeemed. God loves you so much that He wants to bring you into His family and gives you His name, no matter what you have gone through. When you have trusted in Christ, you are a child of the King.

You are adopted and baptized into the family of the One who created the heavens and the earth.

You bear His image

Abuse survivors may believe the lie that they are damaged goods, broken, unfixable, unlovely. The lies of their offender and the enemy of their souls ring in their ears, telling them that they're worthless, they're filthy, they're ugly. Because of what man's sin has tried to do to God's beautiful creation, some survivors even grow to hate themselves. But the truth is that the Shepherd of your soul is not ashamed of your wounds and scars. He loves every one of them. God loves to make beauty out of ashes, glory out of mourning, and wholeness out of brokenness, no matter what you have experienced. The truth is that every Christian, no matter how wounded or scarred, has not only been adopted into God's family but also bears HIs beautiful image. Romans 8:29 reminds us that God's desire is for HIs children "to be conformed to the image of HIs Son." Second Corinthians 3:18 says, "We all, with unveiled face, beholding as in a mirror the glory of the Lord, are being transformed into the same image from glory to glory, just as by the Spirit of the Lord." God is in the process of transforming HIs children into HIs own image, and this includes you. He loves you. He wants to help you become more like Him each day of your Christian life.

> *What an important point this is! Hearing over and over that I am an image bearer and that my abusers have done great harm against an image bearer of Christ makes it sound like it really means something to God, and like I belong to him. It finally*

becomes possible for me to see why he might care about me, at least as an image bearer. It's a place to start.[213]

You are spiritually alive and can walk in the power of the Spirit

In Ephesians 2:1 Paul says, "And you [who trusted in Him] he made alive, who were dead in trespasses and sins." He goes on in that passage to remind you that God in HIs great love and mercy intervened to change your condition. He made you "alive together with Christ," raised you up spiritually, and made you able to "sit together in heavenly places in Christ Jesus,"[214] as citizens of heaven. What a contrast to the kingdom of darkness we came from!

Paul goes on to say in verse 7 that God has done this so that in the ages to come, He can "show the exceeding riches of his grace in his kindness toward us in Christ Jesus." Not only are the Father and the Son looking forward to your being with them in heaven, but God will shower His people with kindness for all of eternity. The abuse will be long forgotten, the rejection, the humiliation, the nightmares will never again come into your mind, but you will enjoy being with Jesus, along with all of God's children forever. Sometimes it's hard to see beyond this life on earth with all of its hardships, but one day you will be with your Good Shepherd forever. The eyes of faith have to look beyond the physical world to see the spiritual world that is more real.

When you trust in Christ, your standing before God and your eternal destiny completely change. However, many of life's circumstances are still the same. You still live in a physical body with the effects of sin that have not yet been lifted from this earth. You become

---

213   Personal correspondence, used by permission.

214   Ephesians 2:1–6.

entirely clean and new on the inside because you have been made alive spiritually by the power of the Holy Spirit, but for now you still reside in a fleshly body that is subject to decay. The eyes of faith have to look beyond the physical world to see the spiritual world that is more real.

> Therefore we do not lose heart. Even though our outward man is perishing, yet the inward man is being renewed day by day. For our light affliction, which is but for a moment, is working for us a far more exceeding and eternal weight of glory, while we do not look at the things which are seen, but at the things which are not seen. For the things which are seen are temporary, but the things which are not seen are eternal.[215]

Paul said in Romans 8:18, "For I consider that the sufferings of this present time are not worthy to be compared with the glory which shall be revealed in us." God is not making light of our sufferings, but He wants us to see our sufferings in light of eternity, when all pain and suffering will be forgotten. Revelation 21:4 tells us, "God will wipe away every tear from their eyes; there shall be no more death, nor sorrow, nor crying. There shall be no more pain, for the former things have passed away."

MOVE FORWARD WITH THE SHEPHERD OF YOUR SOUL

In Luke 15, Jesus told the parable of the lost sheep, whom the Good Shepherd went out to find. In John 10, Jesus described Himself

---

215   2 Corinthians 4:16–18.

as that Good Shepherd, who gives His life for the sheep. One abuse survivor who began to understand this truth wrote:

> I've grown up with the Bible pretty much only used as a weapon to humiliate, to manipulate, etc. Growing up, that always worked, until I realized that it was impossible to please that god. At the time, instead of realizing and understanding that God had prepared a way for me, I turned away, thinking there was no hope of pleasing him.
>
> When I came to my church, it was the first time that I saw that perhaps I could live in a way that pleased him—not through my own works, but through Jesus. Initially, I reacted in terror. I didn't want to hope. The concept of God loving me was something that brought fear. Love to me meant slavery and manipulation, and hope could bring more pain than just about anything else. I didn't want to take any more risks.
>
> In time though, I learned it was something real and true. Much of what God taught me was through the people of God who were around me, perhaps a pale reflection of him, but still a reflection. God used them to draw me to himself. He used them to paint a picture of himself for my heart. I look back at some of the people he used at that time. They weren't special in and of themselves. They just loved with the love that God had poured into them. It was the first time that I saw that God could really look at me and be pleased—not because of me, but because of the gift he had provided. That was all very shocking, humbling, overwhelming.

I wanted to yell and shout, sing and dance (albeit without any coordination at all)! I felt like I couldn't hold the joy and freedom that belonged to me because of what Jesus did. I was overwhelmingly thankful and loved him. My love came from the small picture I was given of his love. The glimpse I was given was overwhelming to me and just resulted in my loving him back. Mine was a bit of a broken love, sometimes fearful, wanting constant reassurance that it was all really true, but also kind of overwhelming. That he could really love me was shocking. I KNEW that I didn't deserve it. I KNEW that I didn't have anything to offer him. I was overwhelmed that knowing that, he still wanted me.[216]

Romans 5:2 tells us that through Jesus Christ, "we have access by faith into this grace in which we stand, and rejoice in hope of the glory of God." Stand in that grace in Christ, even if you feel battered and broken, and trust God to strengthen your faith. If you're falling on rock bottom, the rock that you fall on is the Solid Rock of Jesus Christ, and there's no better place for your hope to be founded.

In the power of the Holy Spirit, walking with the Shepherd of your soul, you can move forward toward victory. It may be a long road, and you will want loving, compassionate others around you, but He has called you out of darkness and into His marvelous light.

Just as Lazarus, with the help of others, shed his grave clothes,[217] you can shed those lies one by one like old rags, and walk in the light of His truth. Walk with your hand in the hand of the Shepherd of your soul.

---

216   Personal correspondence, used by permission.
217   The story of Jesus raising Lazarus from the dead is found in John 11.

CHAPTER 14

VOICES OF GRIEF, VOICES OF HOPE

LORD, how long will the wicked,

How long will the wicked triumph?

They utter speech, and speak insolent things;

All the workers of iniquity boast in themselves.

They break in pieces your people, O Lord,

And afflict your heritage.

They slay the widow and the stranger

And murder the fatherless.

Yet they say, "The Lord does not see,

Nor does the God of Jacob understand."

Who will rise up for me against the evildoers?

Who will stand up for me against the workers of iniquity?

Unless the LORD had been my help,

My soul would soon have settled in silence.

If I say, "My foot slips,"

Your mercy, O Lord, will hold me up.

In the multitude of my anxieties within me,

Your comforts delight my soul.[218]

---

218   Psalm 94:3–7, 16–19.

I sat on a stool on the church platform, listening to Scott Krippayne sing "What Breaks Your Heart."

Don't want to be numb to injustice . . .
Don't want to get used to the evil I see . . . [219]

It was the summer of 2012. Seven years had passed since the beginning of our pilgrimage into understanding the dynamics of abuse. I felt far more than seven years older.

With the help of our small church, Faith and I had begun our ministry, Speaking Truth in Love, traveling, telling our own story, alerting churches and schools to the very real need in their midst to confront the offenders and enablers, and to help the victims of abuse, even years after the abuse had taken place.

During the course of our traveling and speaking, we had heard stories from many abuse survivors. Often the people who spoke with us were coming forward with their story for the very first time. So many of them held a common theme. Their abuse had been hidden. Their offender had been protected. They had felt shamed and blamed.

Many of them said that what drove them away from church, and sometimes even from God, was not the initial abuse itself, as horrific as that was. Rather, it was the response of the church.

Faith and I had read stacks of books over the last seven years. But the one I was thinking about right now, sitting on that platform,

---

219   Scott Krippayne, "What Breaks Your Heart," (Spring Hill Music Group, 2006).

was Christa Brown's book, This Little Light. *The tragic story of an entire denomination's stonewalling of her efforts for truth and justice and protection for the vulnerable.*

No church leader "ever even had the decency to look me in the face and say 'We're so sorry,'" she had written.[220]

No one ever said they were sorry.

But today was going to be different. Today we were saying we were sorry.

During the course of our traveling and speaking, while we met one person after another who told a story of abuse, it so happened that we met two sisters who had been abused by someone in our very own church, forty years earlier. That abuser had become a deacon in the church. The sisters had never been helped.

No one had ever said they were sorry.

Now I was the pastor of Curtis Baptist Church. As a church, together, we were together saying we were sorry. We were grieving together. A Service of Lament.

> If you and I are to know each other in a deep way, we must not only share our hurts, anger, and disappointment with each other (which we often do), we must also lament them together before the God who hears and is moved by our tears. Only then does our sharing become truly redemptive in character. The degree to which I am willing to enter into the suffering of another person reveals the level of my

---

220 Brown, *This Little Light,* p. 129.

commitment and love for them. If I am not interested in your hurts, I am not really interested in you.[221]

It was a Sunday afternoon. I didn't know how many people would come, but I had been describing this day from the pulpit for months. It was a plan we'd been discussing, forming for at least four years, ever since the sisters, who now lived in different states, had first spoken to us.

Fewer than fifty people filled the pews, but I was satisfied. This wasn't a service for gawkers. It was a time for people to gather who joined us in saying, "We're so sorry. We want to weep with you. We want to stand with you."

"That's a big part of lamenting as a church together—basically showing up."[222]

I spoke about our own journey. I read quotations from Christa Brown. We listened to MercyMe sing "When the Hurt and the Healer Collide."[223]

Then I spoke from Matthew 18, when our Lord Jesus talked about the little children, anger and grief welling up in me. "The one who causes the offenses, he is the one to blame," I said. "All the little ones who are offended are blameless in the eyes of God." I thought of the many people who had been abused, wondering

---

221   Card, *A Sacred Sorrow*, p. 29.

222   Michael Card, quoted in "Bringing Our Pain to God: Michael Card and Calvin Seerveld on biblical lament in worship," by Steve and Joan Huyser-Honig, accessed at http://worship.calvin.edu/resources/resource-library/bringing-our-pain-to-god-michael-card-and-calvin-seerveld-on-biblical-lament-in-worship/.

223   Bart Millard, Robby Shaffer, Jim Bryson. Mike Schuechzer. Nathan Cochran, Barry Graul, "The Hurt and the Healer" (MercyMe, 2012).

where their churches were in their time of need, wondering where the church was even now.

So many of them were still lost, like the lost lambs that the Shepherd went out to find. He was seeking those ones who had been offended against.

After I spoke, Faith told her own story of abuse and silence and speaking and healing. Then one of the sisters spoke, one who had been abused forty years earlier. There were tears, and we were unashamed.

We're so sorry.

Then we opened the service for anyone else to speak who wanted to. We weren't here to provide answers. We were here to feel the sorrow. To mourn. We didn't know if anyone else would speak. We sat quietly, listening to the music.

But they came. One after another. They wanted to break the silence and tell their stories.

The other sister came, the other one who had been abused forty years earlier. She had brought her adult children, who were hearing their mother's and aunt's story for the first time.

Then another. "I was raped by a guest speaker at our church when I was little. For years I thought I was going to hell."

Another. "I was molested when I went to my pastor for counseling."

More and more. So many tears.

We love you, and we're so, so sorry. We weep with you.

A lament involves the energy to search, not to shut down the quest for truth. It is passion to ask, rather than to rant and rave with already reached conclusions. A lament uses the language of pain, anger, and confusion and moves toward God.[224]

We listened to Steve Siler sing "Innocent Child."

Oh precious one, I know the nightmares you've had
Don't be ashamed. You didn't do anything bad. . . .
It's not your fault. You are an innocent child.[225]

At the end, we held out white roses for all who wanted one. A symbol of your innocence, that all guilt and shame and blame for the offense lay at the feet of the offender. You were not at fault. You were innocent and blameless in God's eyes. The Shepherd of your souls loves you dearly.

A large candle stood in the center of the table. Around it stood small candles in heart-shaped dishes.

You are dearly loved.

Anyone who wished could come to the front and light a small candle from the large one.

We will shine together as lights.

We stood together. Weeping together. Holding out our candles.

---

224   Dan Allender, "The Hidden Hope in Lament," *Mars Hill Review,* premier issue, 1994, pp. 25-38.

225   Steve Siler, "Innocent Child," (Fifty States Music, 1990).

We will stand with you. We will not be silent. We will speak the truth.

We don't need to be afraid to weep without providing a quick solution. This is a time for tears. Hope will follow.

> Lament opens the heart to wrestle with a God who knows
> that sorrow leads to comfort and lament moves to praise as
> sure as the crucifixion gave way to resurrection.[226]

We will wrestle with God and cry out to God.

So let us weep. Let us pray.

Let us be wise to perceive and respond to evil.

We will trust in the Shepherd who promised to find the lost sheep.

Let us open our hearts. Let us love fully.

Let us run to help and comfort the most vulnerable among us.

We will hope in His eventual triumph over evil.

We will believe the truth.

So let us speak the truth.

Let us Tear Down This Wall of Silence.

---

226 Dan Allender, "The Hidden Hope in Lament."

SELECTED BIBLIOGRAPHY

Allender, Dr. Dan B. "The Hidden Hope in Lament," *Mars Hill Review*, premier issue, 1994, pp. 25-38, accessed via http://www.leaderu.com/marshill/mhro1/lament1.html.

Allender, Dr. Dan B. *The Wounded Heart: Hope for Adult Victims of Childhood Sexual Abuse.* Colorado Springs: NavPress, 2008.

Anderson, Bill. *When Child Abuse Comes to Church: Recognizing Its Occurrence and What to Do About It.* Minneapolis: Bethany House, 1992.

Annis, Ann W; Michelle Loyd-Paige; Rodger R. Rice. *Set Us Free: What the Church Needs to Know from Survivors of Abuse.* New York: Calvin College Social Research Center and University Press of America, Inc., 2001.

Brown, Christa. *This Little Light: Beyond a Baptist Preacher Predator and His Gang.* Cedarburg, WI: Foremost Press, 2009.

Card, Michael. *A Sacred Sorrow: Reaching Out to God in the Lost Language of Lament.* Colorado Springs: NavPress, 2005.

Cloud, Dr. Henry; Dr. John Townsend. *Boundaries: When to Say Yes How to Say No to Take Control of Your Life.* Grand Rapids: Zondervan, 2002.

Crewdson, John. *By Silence Betrayed: Sexual Abuse of Children in America*. Boston: Little, Brown and Company, 1988.

Crippen, Jeff and Anna Wood. *A Cry for Justice: How the Evil of Domestic Abuse Hides in Your Church!* Greenville, SC: Calvary Press Publishing, 2012.

Crough, Patrick. *The Serpents among Us: How to Protect Your Children from Sexual Predators—A Police Investigator's Perspective*. Millstone Justice, 2009.

DeMuth, Mary. *Not Marked: Finding Hope and Healing after Sexual Abuse*. Uncaged Publishing, 2013.

Feuereisen, Patti. *Invisible Girls: The Truth about Sexual Abuse*. Berkeley: Seal Press, 2002.

Glover, Voyle. *Protecting Your Church against Sexual Predators*. Grand Rapids: Kregel Publications, 2005.

Heffernan, Margaret. *Willful Blindness: Why We Ignore the Obvious at Our Peril*. New York: Walker & Company, 2012.

Heitritter, Lynn and Jeanette Vought. *Helping Victims of Sexual Abuse: A Sensitive Biblical Guide for Counselors, Victims, and Families*. Minneapolis: Bethany House, 2006.

Herman, Judith Lewis. *Trauma and Recovery: The Aftermath of Violence—from Domestic Abuse to Political Terror*. Basic Books, 1997.

Holcomb, Justin and Lindsey Holcomb. *Rid of My Disgrace: Hope and Healing for Victims of Sexual Assault*. Wheaton, IL: Crossway Publishers, 2011.

Hurnard, Hannah. *Hinds' Feet on High Places*. Colchester, UK: Christian Literature Crusade, 1955.

Johnson, David and Jeff VanVonderen. *The Subtle Power of Spiritual Abuse: Recognizing and Escaping Spiritual Manipulation and False Spiritual Authority within the Church.* Minneapolis: Bethany House, 2005.

Johnson, Victoria L. *Children and Sexual Abuse.* Downers Grove, IL: InterVarsity Press, 2007.

Johnson, Victoria L. *Restoring Broken Vessels: Confronting the Attack on Female Sexuality.* IVP Books, 2002.

Langberg, Diane, Ph.D. *On the Threshold of Hope: Opening the Door to Healing for Survivors of Sexual Abuse.* Carol Stream, Illinois: Tyndale House Publishers, Inc., 1999.

Langberg, Diane, Ph.D. "Clergy Sexual Abuse," in C. C. Kroeger and J.R. Beck, eds, *Abuse, Women, and the Bible* (Grand Rapids: Baker Books, 1996) accessed via http://www.dianelangberg.com/work/articles/ClergySexualAbuse.pdf.

Langberg, Diane, Ph.D. "Coping with Traumatic Memory." *Marriage and Family: a Christian Journal.* 5(4), pp. 447-456.

Langberg, Diane, Ph.D. *Counseling Survivors of Sexual Abuse.* Xulon Press, 2003.

Maltz, Wendy. *The Sexual Healing Journey.* New York: HarperCollins Publishers, 2012.

Massi, Jeri. *Schizophrenic Christianity: How Christian Fundamentalism Attracts and Protects Sociopaths, Abusive Pastors, and Child Molesters.* Jupiter Rising Books, 2014.

Pakkala, Alaine. *Laura: A True Story.* Camp Hill, PA: Christian Publications, 2002.

Reju, Deepak. *On Guard: Preventing and Responding to Child Abuse.* Greensboro: New Growth Press, 2014.

Rodriguez, Kathy D., Psy.D. and Pam W. Vredevelt. *Surviving the Secret: Healing the Hurts of Sexual Abuse.* CreateSpace Independent Publishing Platform, 2013.

Salter, Anna C., Ph.D. *Transforming Trauma: A Guide to Understanding and Treating Adult Survivors.* New York: Sage Publications, Inc., 1995.

Salter, Anna C., Ph.D. *Predators: Pedophiles, Rapists and Other Sex Offenders.* New York: Basic Books, 2003.

Stafford, Wes. *Too Small to Ignore: Why the Least of These Matters Most.* Colorado Springs: Waterbrook Press, 2007.

Stout, Martha, Ph.D. *The Sociopath Next Door.* New York: Three Rivers, 2005.

Sumpter, Toby J. *Job Through New Eyes: A Son for Glory.* Monroe, LA: Athanasius Press, 2012.

Vernick, Leslie. *The Emotionally Destructive Marriage: How to Find Your Voice and Reclaim Your Hope.* Waterbrook Press, 2013.

Vieth, Victor I; Bette L. Bottoms and Alison Perona. *Ending Child Abuse: New Efforts in Prevention, Investigation, and Training.* London: Routledge, 2005.

Welch, Edward T. *Shame Interrupted: How God Lifts the Pain of Worthlessness and Rejection.* Greensboro, NC: New Growth Press, 2012.

Wilder, E. James; Edward M. Khouri; Chris M. Coursey; and Shelia D. Sutton. *Joy Starts Here: the transformation zone.* East Peoria, IL: Shepherd's House Inc., 2013.

OTHER RESOURCES

In addition to the books listed in the bibliography, you may find these organizations, websites, books, and other resources helpful.

For more education about abuse and its effects

Rape, Abuse, and Incest National Network (RAINN), www.rainn.org

Global Trauma Recovery, www.globaltraumarecovery.org

The Report of the investigation of New Tribes Mission conducted by the organization Godly Response to Abuse in the Christian Environment. "Amended GRACE Report on NTM Fanda." https://www.scribd.com/doc/36559323/Amended-GRACE-Report-on-NTM-Fanda-Amended-Edition.

All God's Children, a film about abuse at a missionary boarding school. www.allgodschildrenthefilm.com

Audio documentaries about abuse in children's homes, www.jeriwho.net/documentaries

Godly Response to Abuse in the Christian Environment, www.netgrace.org

To bring accountability to churches and Christian ministries

Godly Response to Abuse in the Christian Environment, www.netgrace.org

The Survivor Network of Those Abused by Priests and Other Clergy, www.snapnetwork.org

Blog on the Way lists sexual abusers in the fundamentalist context who have been arrested, www.jeriwho.net/lillypad2

A Cry for Justice, website of Jeff Crippen, author of the book by the same name, www.cryingoutforjustice.com

To help churches and families learn how to protect their vulnerable ones

Speaking Truth in Love Ministries (Dale and Faith Ingraham), www.speakingtruthinlove.org

Plan to Protect, www.winningkidsinc.ca

Godly Response to Abuse in the Christian Environment, www.netgrace.org

Darkness to Light, www.d2l.org

Ministry Safe, www.ministrysafe.com

For parents with small children

I Said No! A kid-to-kid guide to keeping your private parts private by Kimberly King

No Trespassing: This is MY Body by Pattie Fitzgerald and Safely Ever After, Inc. www.safelyeverafter.com.

The Swimsuit Lesson by Jon Holsten, www.swimsuitlesson.com

Not with My Child, www.notwithmychild.org

For seminars, conferences, connections, and other resources to help abuse survivors

MKSafetyNet, for "missionary kid" survivors, www.mksafetynet.net

Male Survivor, www.malesurvivor.org.

Living Waters Ministries, www.desertstream.org

Restoration in Christ Ministries, www.rcm-usa.org

Mending the Soul, www.mendingthesoul.org

His Healing Light Ministries, www.hishealinglight.org

The Hope of Survivors, www.thehopeofsurvivors.com

Jim Wilder, author of *Joy Starts Here,* has done much work on the power of joy. www.lifemodel.org, www.joystartshere.com, www.thrivingrecovery.org, www.thrivetoday.org

For survivors meeting in small groups, books with a workbook component

Boundaries: When to Say Yes How to Say No to Take Control of Your Life, by Dr. Henry Cloud and Dr. John Townsend

Joy Starts Here: the transformation zone, by E. James Wilder, Edward M. Khouri, Chris M. Coursey, and Shelia D. Sutton

Mending the Soul: Understanding and Healing Abuse, by Steven R. Tracy

Not Marked: Finding Hope and Healing after Sexual Abuse, by Mary DeMuth

On the Threshold of Hope: Opening the Door to Healing for Survivors of Sexual Abuse, by Diane Langberg, Ph.D.

Rapha's Touch: Healing from Sexual Abuse, by JoAnne Streeter Shade

Surviving the Secret: Healing the Hurts of Sexual Abuse, by Kathy D. Rodriguez, Psy.D. and Pam W. Vredevelt

The Wounded Heart: Hope for Adult Victims of Childhood Sexual Abuse, by Dr. Dan B. Allender

For repentant offenders

Pure Life Ministries, www.purelifeministries.org

Broken Yoke Ministries, www.brokenyoke.org

GENERAL INDEX

SCRIPTURE INDEX

"Dale Ingraham and Rebecca Davis have written a well researched resource for believers navigating sexual abuse in their churches or ministries. Proverbs 17:15 says that those who justify the wicked and condemn the just are both abominations to the Lord. It is of utmost importance that the Church reflect God's heart for justice on this issue. This book is a readable, accessible tool for educating our congregations to that end."

—Wendy Alsup, author and founder,
Practical Theology for Women and *The Gospel-Centered Woman*
www.theologyforwomen.org | www.gospelcenteredwoman.com

"*Tear Down This Wall of Silence* is both a command and a comfort. Those tempted to cloak the crimes of sexual abuse in a shroud of secrecy will be convinced there's no other way to stop this awful epidemic than to tear down the wall of silence behind which abusers and enablers hide. For victims of sexual abuse, it serves as a balm to the wounded soul. It's a book I wish I didn't have to recommend, but after reading it I know that I must and that I will."

—Wade Burleson, pastor, blogger, and author,
Happiness Doesn't Just Happen and *Hard Ball Religion*
www.wadeburleson.com

"As one who has witnessed first hand the devastation of the mishandling of sexual abuse in a church context, I'm elated to see this much needed resource for the Church. I pray it gets into the hands of every pastor and church leader, so that the safety and well-being of the vulnerable and the wounded can be given the same priority that Christ Himself gave."

—Kristi Kernal, OAASIS: Oregon Abuse
Advocates & Survivors in Service
www.oaasisoregon.org

"Compassionate, biblical, and hopeful . . . *Tear Down This Wall of Silence* is a passionate cry on behalf of those who have lost their voices."

—Urisou Brito, pastor and Chair of Committee on Child
Protection, Communion of Reformed Evangelical Churches

For more information about

Tear Down This Wall of Silence
&
Dale Ingraham
please visit:

www.speakingtruthinlove.org
dfingraham@speakingtruthinlove.org
www.facebook.com/SpeakingTruthInLove

For more information about
AMBASSADOR INTERNATIONAL
please visit:

www.ambassador-international.com
@AmbassadorIntl
www.facebook.com/AmbassadorIntl